God on Climate Change

Change

Worshipping creation instead of the Creator

Jim Wear

ISBN 978-0-692-97823-8
Publisher: Lifelinz Publishing—Smithfield, NC
Library of Congress Card Control Number: 2017918575
Wear, Jim
God on Climate Change/ Wear, Jim
Available Formats: eBook | Paperback distribution

DEDICATION

Dedicated to the strongest person I know, my wife, Debbie. Without you, this book would not have come to fruition. To those who inspired it and will not read it because you have fallen prey to the "global warming" propaganda, I thank you as well.

INTRODUCTION

A tax on air? Seems like a joke but that is exactly what proponents of "climate change," the new catch phrase that has morphed from "global warming," propose in order to save the earth from annihilation. Science is inconclusive on "global warming" because the earth will always go through its promised cycles of Genesis 8:22, *"While the earth remains, seedtime and harvest, cold and heat, winter and summer, and day and night shall not cease."*

So while the summer produces heat waves, melting ice and the occasional hurricane, "global warming" fits in nicely with the agenda to save the earth. But then when winter comes, as it always does, with its record snow storms and freezing cold, "global warming" is no longer a viable explanation. Ah yes, let's call it "climate change" and still blame it on mankind.

Folks, man-made "global warming," a.k.a. "climate change," is simply an opinion based on computer models, which in turn is based on data entered into the computer by man. For every scientist who claims man is causing climate change, you can find another claiming it is a hoax. Why? That is because there is no conclusive evidence that man can affect the overall ecological effects of the earth, let alone the expanse of the universe. If there was proof, everyone would be on board with the scientific evidence and the debate would be settled. For example, photosynthesis from trees, plants, algae, etc. uses carbon dioxide (the air we exhale) and water to produce sugars from which other organic compounds can be constructed, and oxygen (the air we inhale) is produced as a by-product. That is a fact all agree on and not an opinion.

So what does God have to say about "climate change?" A lot, actually. It is time we heed what the word of God, the Bible, discloses about creation and the Creator. To be blunt, "climate change" is born out of idolatry. It is the environmentalists who worship creation over the Creator. While we are to be good stewards of the earth, we lose sight that we also are His creation. *"But now, O LORD, You are our Father; we are the clay, and You our potter; and all we are the work of Your hand"* (Isaiah 64:8).

As you read this book, ask yourself this question. Why would a Creator, God, create mankind to inhabit His creation knowing that man has the power to destroy His creation? It is illogical and absurd on its face. The "climate change" movement has become a religion based on emotion, ignorance, propaganda and monetary agendas. It is time to set the record straight. Job 12:10 ask, "*In whose hand is the life of every living thing, and the breath of all mankind?*" God was, is and will always be in control of His creation, and that includes you and me.

Ask God for wisdom when reading His word so you are no longer ignorant concerning this topic. "*If any of you lacks wisdom, let him ask of God, who gives to all liberally and without reproach, and it will be given to him*" (James 1:5). Now let's expose His truth and may God bless you as you read.

Chapter One
Creator

"*In the beginning God created the heavens and the earth*" (Genesis 1:1). If one digs deeper into this first verse of God's word, you will have a whole new outlook toward creation and its Creator. We will discuss the heavens and the earth in the next chapter but let's explore the genesis of everything we see and … don't see. More specifically, "In the beginning God!"

Who is God? Let's connect the dots according to scripture. "*For there are three that bear witness in heaven: the Father, the Word, and the Holy Spirit; and these three are one*" (1 John 5:7). God is first our Father in heaven. The Holy Spirit is also God. He makes his first appearance in scripture in verse two of Genesis: "*And the Spirit of God was hovering over the face of the waters.*" Today, the Holy Spirit lives inside each believer of Christ. "*But if the Spirit of Him who raised Jesus from the dead dwells in you, He who raised Christ from the dead will also give life to your mortal bodies through*

His Spirit who dwells in you" (Romans 8:11). And that brings us to "the Word" – the reason why creation exists.

"The Word" is also God. Take note that "the Word" is one with "the Father" and "the Holy Spirit." How can three distinct manifestations (forms of an individual) be one entity? The best way I know how to explain the "trinity" concept is to use H_2O in place of God. H_2O is the chemical formula for water, ice or steam; three forms but the same core substance. God is therefore the Father, the Word, and the Holy Spirit. Now we are getting to the reason why creation exists.

"*In the beginning was the Word, and the Word was with God, and the Word was God. He was in the beginning with God. All things were made through Him, and without Him nothing was made that was made*" (John 1:1-3). Wow! Note that "the Word" was with God, and is God, from the very beginning in Genesis 1:1 and that creation was made because of Him. Again this confirms the three in one concept. "*And the Word became flesh and dwelt among us, and we beheld His glory, the glory as of the only begotten of the Father, full of grace and truth*" (John 1:14). The dots keep connecting. Jesus Christ said, "*I and My Father are*

2

one" (John 10:30) and "*I am the way, the truth, and the life. No one comes to the Father except through Me*" (John 14:6). The truth is Jesus. The way is Jesus. Eternal life is through Jesus. The Word is Jesus. Jesus is God and the reason why our Creator, the Father, made everything.

"*He is the image of the invisible God, the firstborn over all creation. For by Him all things were created that are in heaven and that are on earth, visible and invisible, whether thrones or dominions or principalities or powers. All things were created through Him and for Him. And He is before all things, and in Him all things consist. And He is the head of the body, the church, who is the beginning, the firstborn from the dead, that in all things He may have the preeminence*" (Colossians 1:15-18). Double wow! Jesus is the firstborn over all creation (the only begotten of the Father), meaning He is before all things and the reason why creation exists and coexists. He is also the firstborn from the dead after being crucified on the cross. The significance of that event cannot be overstated because His death and resurrection is the basis for mankind's salvation. Thus Jesus is the beginning of all creation, in its perfect state, and the beginning of salvation to make "all things" perfect again. The dots are now connected, but let's drive the point home so you get the totality of why all creation exists.

"*For us there is one God, the Father, of whom are all things, and we for Him; and one Lord Jesus Christ, through whom are all things, and through whom we live*" (1 Corinthians 8:6). Creation is the clay and He is the potter. All things exist because of the Father, our Creator, but through His Son, Jesus Christ. "*It is He who sits above the circle of the earth, and its inhabitants are like grasshoppers, who stretches out the heavens like a curtain, and spreads them out like a tent to dwell in*" (Isaiah 40:22). God dwells in heaven, above the earth and we are like insects hopping around His creation. Can you picture a large wheat field full of grasshoppers? That is God's view from above concerning mankind. "*He has made the earth by His power, He has established the world by His wisdom, and has stretched out the heavens at His discretion*" (Jeremiah 10:12). By power and wisdom the earth was made and everything in it. Creation is no accident or some cosmic coincidence! King David put musical notes to this absolute truth: "*The Lord, Who made heaven and earth*" (Psalm 115:15; 121:2; 124:8 & 134:3).

"*He was in the world, and the world was made through Him, and the world did not know Him*" (John 1:10). That would be Jesus, conceived by

4

the Holy Spirit (Matthew 1:20), born of a virgin (Isaiah 7:14), 100% man and 100% God, whom the world rejected (even His own people) and crucified. His shed sinless blood on the cross and subsequent death paid a debt He did not owe (1 Corinthians 6:20) so that we, mankind, can be restored to a right relationship with God, the Father. The Man who knew no sin (2 Corinthians 5:21) bore all our sins (1 Peter 2:24) because the wages of sin is death (Romans 6:23). The resurrection of Jesus from the grave was the final nail (pun intended since nails were used to crucify Jesus) in the coffin for Satan. It is finished (John 19:30)! The future home of Satan, the devil, is the lake of fire (Revelation 20:10). Unfortunately that is also the future home of many who choose not to believe in the name of Jesus Christ (Revelation 19:20; 20:15) and accept His sacrifice for their sins (Hebrews 10:12). They will pay the death penalty on their own in this life and the next (the second death). The above is vital to your understanding of creation's purpose.

It is by God's will that creation exists. "*You are worthy, O Lord, to receive glory and honor and power; for You created all things, and by Your will they exist and were created*" (Revelation 4:11). Therefore, one can logically conclude that it is also God's will if He wanted creation to no longer exist. But that brings us to His purpose. Jesus said in Matthew 28:18, "*All authority has been given to Me in heaven and on earth.*" Furthermore, God the Father stated in Hebrews 1:2, "*by His Son, whom He has appointed heir of all things, through whom also He made the worlds.*" Again, creation is no accident! Creation has a purpose. It will one day be inherited by King Jesus and His saints, those who believed in His name as their Savior (1 Thessalonians 3:13; Jude 1:14). That is not possible if mankind has the power to completely destroy the earth.

You may be asking yourself, "Well, I just don't believe in all this God stuff and Jesus." It takes faith. "*So then faith comes by hearing, and hearing by the word of God*" (Romans 10:17). After reading this you no longer have an excuse. "What is faith?" you may be asking. "*Now faith is the substance of things hoped for, the evidence of things not seen*" (Hebrews 11:1). God will give you the faith needed upon believing in His Son, whom you have never seen. Jesus said in John 20:29, "*Blessed are those who have not seen and yet have believed.*" Jesus is the author and finisher of our faith (Hebrews 12:2). "*These things I have written to you who believe in the name of the Son of God, that you may know that you have eternal life, and that you* may continue to believe in the name of the Son of God" (1 John 5:13). The first thing you must do is believe in the name of Jesus, that He died for your sins. God then gives you a measure of faith (Romans 12:3). Then you must continue to believe to the end of your life if Jesus does not return before that appointed time.

But there is more to creation than what we can visibly see. "*For since the creation of the world His invisible attributes are clearly seen, being understood by the things that are made, even His eternal power and Godhead, so that they are without excuse*" (Romans 1:20). What are these invisible attributes? The Creator's eternal power and divine nature. In other words, the created universe reveals there is a Creator and a sense of right and wrong. But the Word, Jesus, strengthens that sense through faith. "*By faith we understand that the worlds were framed by the word of God, so that the things which are seen were not made of things which are visible*" (Hebrews 11:3).

You might then ask yourself, "Well I just don't understand all this?" That's OK. You don't have to understand it all. That is what faith is all about, the evidence of things not seen. "*Have you not known? Have you not heard? The everlasting God, the Lord, the Creator of the ends of the earth, neither faints nor is weary. His understanding is unsearchable*" (Isaiah 40:28). We know that a Man by the name of Jesus Christ existed on this earth, who claimed to be God, rose from the grave on the third day. His body was never brought forth to prove otherwise by His disciples, who turned from being cowards to dying for Him because they saw the resurrected Lord. They were true witnesses as attested in the Bible we read. "*A true witness delivers souls, but a deceitful witness speaks lies*" (Proverbs 14:25). The Romans crucified Him, placed Him in a borrowed tomb (Matthew 27:57-60) and then guarded it so no one could steal the body (Matthew 27:64-66). All that had to happen to stop this thing called "Christianity" from spreading to this day was to produce the dead body of Jesus and the greatest fraud in the history of the world would be over! That could not happen because he arose (Luke 24:1-7), the firstborn from the dead (Revelation 1:5). "*For of Him and through Him and to Him are all things, to whom be glory forever. Amen*" (Romans 11:36).

Chapter Two
Creation

Now that we know why creation exists in chapter one, let's return to Genesis 1:1, "*In the beginning God created the heavens and the earth.*" Creation is no accident and the first verse is full of mathematical perfection. "*All Scripture is given by inspiration of God, and is profitable for doctrine, for reproof, for correction, for instruction in righteousness*" (2 Timothy 3:16). Let's break down the math. Scripture was first penned in the Hebrew language. In the English language, verse one contains ten words. But in Hebrew, there are seven (7) words. "*Then God blessed the seventh day and sanctified it, because in it He rested from all His work which God had created and made*" (Genesis 2:3). Used 603 times (59 times in the book of Revelation alone), the number 7 is the foundation of God's word. Seven is the number of completeness and perfection (both physical and spiritual).

To break down verse one even further, there are twenty-eight (28) Hebrew characters that make up the first verse. Revelation 7:1 reveals "*the four corners of the earth, holding the four winds of the earth.*" Throughout the Bible, the number 4 is associated with the earth and the number 7 with completion. So in summary Genesis 1:1 has seven words and twenty-eight characters. Seven times four is twenty-eight (28), God's creative power of the heavens and earth completed in wisdom, knowledge and perfection. "*The Lord by wisdom founded the earth; by understanding He established the heavens*" (Proverbs 3:19). "*The earth shall be full of the knowledge of the Lord*" (Isaiah 11:9).

Verse one is a declarative supernatural theological bombshell. From there God explains in detail how it came about. Note that man had nothing to do with the creation process, but instead is part of creation itself. "*I have made the earth, and created man on it. I—My hands—stretched out the heavens, and all their host I have commanded*" (Isaiah 45:12). But for mankind to survive on earth, the creation process had a certain order. Without it, life as we know it could not exist. "*This is the history of the heavens and the earth when they were created, in the day that the LORD God made the earth and the heavens, before any plant of the field was in the earth and before any herb of the field had grown*" (Genesis 2:4-

5).

"*And there are three that bear witness on earth: the Spirit, the water, and the blood; and these three agree as one*" (1 John 5:8). As we have read in chapter one, everything is made by, for and through Jesus Christ. It was His innocent blood that bears witness as the ultimate sacrifice for mankind's sin on earth via His crucifixion. In Genesis 1:2, the Spirit of God bears witness with a formless earth made entirely of water. Darkness was the order of a timeless past. But then God said … and all of creation was spoken into existence in six days.

"*God is light and in Him is no darkness at all*" (1 John 1:5). God is the source of all life, with Jesus being the decisively indicative test. Jesus said in John 8:12, "*I am the light of the world. He who follows Me shall not walk in darkness, but have the light of life.*" God Himself was the source of light for the first three days of creation. That light ushered in Day and Night, evening and morning, and time began – the first day. God then separated the waters by a firmament on the second day. Above the firmament the water vaporized and became what is called the first and second Heaven, the first being the atmosphere and the second being outer space. The third heaven is the home of God's throne (2

Corinthians 12:2). Now the earth has a definable round form, a skyline with clouds, and water solely contained below the firmament, comparable to the judgment flood in the days of Noah.

It is worth mentioning here two major points as creation is spoken into existence. One, creation was designed with no curse, which would later come because of sin. And second, everything was made in a ready-to-use aged state so all of creation could thrive and coexist: water, air, land, grass and herbs, trees bearing fruit, sun, moon, stars and all living organisms (animals and mankind). Science overlooks the fact that the earth was already aged in the creation process, just as Adam was made in the image of God as a full-grown man. Creation was designed to last forever, with man living forever in communion with God. With that said you can better understand the wisdom, knowledge and power of God in the creation process. Hebrews 1:10 declares "*You, LORD, in the beginning laid the foundation of the earth, and the heavens are the work of Your hands.*"

Distillation is the process of separating components from a liquid mixture by selective evaporation and condensation. That process took place in Genesis 1:6-7 and the result was

12

carbon dioxide being obtained from the air. Because carbon dioxide is also soluble in water, it occurs naturally in groundwater, rivers, lakes, ice caps, glaciers and seawater. Would God pollute his own creation with a harmful substance that can ultimately destroy it? Of course not! God saw that it was good.

The carbon dioxide created on the second day was needed by what would take place on the third. The third day ushered in land, which in turn forced water to now become seas. The same day produced grass, herbs and trees bearing fruit. "*And out of the ground the Lord God made every tree grow that is pleasant to the sight and good for food. The tree of life was also in the midst of the garden, and the tree of the knowledge of good and evil*" (Genesis 2:9). On the fourth day, God's light gave way to the sun, moon and stars as days would become seasons, in time, years. "*Then God said, 'Let there be lights in the firmament of the heavens to divide the day from the night; and let them be for signs and seasons, and for days and years'*" (Genesis 1:14). Plant life can now thrive from the sun's light energy via photosynthesis using the carbon dioxide distilled from the air, and "*mist went up from the earth and watered the whole face of the ground*" (Genesis 2:6). The wisdom of this creative power produced oxygen needed for all life that moves on earth!

Before we cover what God created from the ground, namely all life that moves, the following body of scripture emphatically rejects the climate change propaganda that mankind can destroy the earth. "*Tremble before Him, all the earth. The world also is firmly established, it shall not be moved*" (1 Chronicles 16:30). "*You who laid the foundations of the earth, so that it should not be moved forever*" (Psalm 104:5). "*One generation passes away, and another generation comes; but the earth abides forever*" (Ecclesiastes 1:4). Once again, it is crystal clear that God knew what He was doing when he created all life that moves to inhabit what is unmovable – the earth! If man could destroy the earth, the implications would not be good. But after the sixth day of creation that included man, "*God saw everything that He had made, and indeed it was very good*" (Genesis 1:31). Not just good, but very good! Now on to life that moves.

Which came first, the chicken or the egg? The answer lies in Genesis 1:21: "*So God created great sea creatures and every living thing that moves, with which the waters abounded, according to their kind, and every winged bird according to its kind.*" The chicken came first, as did all other full-grown living creatures, male and female. "*And God blessed them, saying, 'Be fruitful and multiply'*" (Genesis 1:22). The fifth day concludes with the sixth day doubling down with more carbon dioxide production. Carbon dioxide is produced by all aerobic organisms (an organism that can survive and grow in an oxygenated environment) when they metabolize carbohydrate and lipids to produce energy by respiration. It is returned to water via the gills of fish and to the air via the lungs of air-breathing land animals, including humans. We all learn this basic principle early in school. You inhale oxygen and exhale carbon dioxide. The plants intake the carbon dioxide and release oxygen.

On the sixth day, "*God made the beast of the earth according to its kind, cattle according to its kind, and everything that creeps on the earth according to its kind*" (Genesis 1:25). "*Out of the ground the Lord God formed every beast of the field and every bird of the air*" (Genesis 2:19). It is amusing at best to think man could destroy what God created from nothing. From nothing to something, namely earth ("the ground"), comes forth all moving things that breathe. Can man create something new from nothing? No! First you have to get your own dirt. "*That which has been is what will be, that which is done is what will be done, and there is nothing new under the sun*" (Ecclesiastes 1:9). "*For every house is built by someone, but He who built all things is God*" (Hebrews 3:4). Only God can make a "new" thing. Everything man has made or will make comes from what God created in six days. "*For we brought nothing into this world, and it is certain we can carry nothing out*" (1 Timothy 6:7). More on that subject in a later chapter.

"*Then God said, 'Let Us make man in Our image, according to Our likeness.' So God created man in His own image; in the image of God He created him; male and female He created them*" (Genesis 1:26a, 27). Note the words "Us" and "Our" – meaning Adam ("him") was made in the "image" and "likeness" of the triune God (Father, Son and Holy Spirit), created to live forever as an immortal being. Furthermore, likeness does not mean duplicate (exact copy) because man had the capability (free will) to sin, unlike God, who cannot sin (2 Corinthians 5:21, Hebrews 4:15). "*And the Lord God formed man of the dust of the ground, and breathed into his nostrils the breath of life; and man became a living being*" (Genesis 2:7). Once again that breath of life inhales oxygen, exhales carbon dioxide.

"*Then the rib which the Lord God had taken from man He made into a woman, and He brought her to the man. And Adam said: 'This is now bone of my bones and flesh of my flesh; she shall be called*

16

Woman, because she was taken out of Man.'" (Genesis 2:22-23). Eve came from Adam, made from his image and likeness, also an immortal being with free will. "*For man is not from woman, but woman from man*" (1 Corinthians 11:8).

Once again the Spirit, water and blood bear witness on earth with the creation of mankind (1 John 5:8). "*The Spirit of God has made me, and the breath of the Almighty gives me life*" (Job 33:4). "*All in whose nostrils was the breath of the spirit of life*" (Genesis 7:22). The amount of water in the human body ranges from 50-75% and "*the life of the flesh is in the blood*" (Leviticus 17:11). And thus the sixth day concludes with Eve being the bookend of God's creative power. Adam and Eve had an equal desire to worship their Creator in love and adoration, neither looking at the other as someone to rule over. "*And they were both naked, the man and his wife, and were not ashamed*" (Genesis 2:25). They were of one mind, one flesh and one spirit as husband and wife destined to live forever.

Then comes two major directives given to mankind. "*Then God blessed them, and God said to them, 'Be fruitful and multiply; fill the earth and subdue it; have dominion over the fish of the sea, over the birds of the air, and over every living thing that moves on the earth*'" (Genesis 1:28). To this very day, the creation directives still stand because God's nature, character and will for mankind has not changed. *"For I am the Lord, I do not change"* (Malachi 3:6). *"Every good and perfect gift is from above, coming down from the Father of the heavenly lights, who does not change like shifting shadows"* (James 1:17). The first directive is children, a gift from God. It should be noted that God wanted Adam and Eve to have multiple children, with no pain during childbirth for Eve. *"Behold, children are a heritage from the Lord, the fruit of the womb is a reward"* (Psalm 127:3). The children of Adam and Eve would also have immortality, having full access to the "tree of life" as food and live forever (Genesis 3:22).

After filling the earth, the second directive flies in the face of those who worship creation over the Creator, or more specifically worshipping the earth and animals over mankind. *"The heaven, even the heavens, are the Lord's; but the earth He has given to the children of men"* (Psalm 115:16). The phrase "subdue it; have dominion over" from Genesis 1:28 means to keep or bring into bondage the earth while ruling over all animal life that moves. *"I have made the earth, the man and the beast that are on the ground, by My great power and by My outstretched arm, and have given it to whom it seemed proper to Me"*

(Jeremiah 27:5). Any policy or law that promotes the earth or any living thing over mankind's well-being is paganism and is contrary to God's directive. More on that subject later in another chapter.

This brings to mind two obvious questions. First, did God give away His ownership of creation when He instructed man to subdue the earth and have dominion over animal life? *"Indeed heaven and the highest heavens belong to the Lord your God, also the earth with all that is in it"* (Deuteronomy 10:14). *"The earth is the Lord's, and all its fullness, the world and those who dwell therein"* (Psalm 24:1). *"The heavens are Yours, the earth also is Yours; the world and all its fullness, You have founded them"* (Psalm 89:11). The obvious answer to the question is "No." As Exodus 19:5 states, *"for all the earth is Mine."*

Secondly, did God expect man to treat the earth and animal life irresponsibly? To the contrary. All life was vegetarian from the beginning and lived in harmony with each other without fear. *"And God said, 'See, I have given you every herb that yields seed which is on the face of all the earth, and every tree whose fruit yields seed; to you it shall be for food. Also, to every beast of the earth, to every bird of the air, and to everything that creeps on the earth, in which there is life, I have given*

19

every green herb for food" (Genesis 1:29-30). The lion could lay with the lamb beside Adam and eat herbs for food. Moreover, God gave Adam a charge which he failed to do and as a result sin entered the world through him, not Eve. *"Therefore, just as through one man sin entered the world, and death through sin, and thus death spread to all men, because all sinned"* (Romans 5:12). That charge still stands today. What is it?

"Before any plant of the field was in the earth and before any herb of the field had grown. For the Lord God had not caused it to rain on the earth, and there was no man to till the ground; but a mist went up from the earth and watered the whole face of the ground" (Genesis 2:5-6). *"Then the Lord God took the man and put him in the garden of Eden to tend and keep it"* (Genesis 2:15). The words "till" and "tend" have the same Hebrew root meaning, to work and labor. Even more specific, to serve another by labor. Adam was also to "keep" the garden, meaning he was to guard, observe, have charge of, keep watch and ward, protect and save life. He was the first watchman! He failed miserably at the task because Eve was tempted by the serpent in the garden (Genesis 3:1).

For the purpose of this chapter, man's charge is to protect God's creation. The problem with environmentalism and paganism is that people have taken good stewardship, as charged by our Creator, and turned it into worshipping the earth and/or animals over mankind. That is idolatry. Lastly, it is not possible for mankind to destroy creation since he and she are a part of it. Can we pollute it? Yes. Can we clean it up? Yes. Can we control nature? No. Can we destroy the earth in its entirety? No! *"You alone are the Lord; You have made heaven, the heaven of heavens, with all their host, the earth and everything on it, the seas and all that is in them, and You preserve them all. The host of heaven worships You"* (Nehemiah 9:6). *"For thus says the Lord, Who created the heavens, Who is God, Who formed the earth and made it, Who has established it, Who did not create it in vain, Who formed it to be inhabited: 'I am the Lord, and there is no other'"* (Isaiah 45:18). God did not create the earth in vain. It was perfectly designed to be inhabited by all living things. There was no death. *"His work is perfect"* (Deuteronomy 32:4). *"His way is perfect"* (2 Samuel 22:31; Psalm 18:30). It was simply perfect!

Chapter Three
Cursed

Choices have consequences. *"And the Lord God commanded the man, saying, 'Of every tree of the garden you may freely eat; but of the tree of the knowledge of good and evil you shall not eat, for in the day that you eat of it you shall surely die'"* (Genesis 2:16-17). A command is handed down by God to man (Hebrew root name for Adam) that if you do this one thing, "you shall surely die." Adam was smart enough to understand that death was some kind of punishment for disobedience, even though he had not experienced it. In Genesis 2:9 we are told about two specific trees: the "tree of life" that is only for those granted eternal life (Genesis 3:22; Revelation 2:7; 22:2, 14) and the "tree of the knowledge of good and evil" that leads to death. God told Adam that he could freely eat from every tree, which included the "tree of life," but do not eat from the "tree of death" (quotes added to point out the two options). Innocence and immortality would soon be shattered by one man. Additionally, all of creation was created through, for and by Jesus Christ (Colossians 1:16), and served as a backdrop for a bigger purpose – good versus evil. That purpose will be discussed in the last chapter.

When God put Adam in the garden of Eden to tend and keep it along with instructions not to eat from the tree of knowledge, Eve did not exist. Remember the game where someone whispers in your ear what to say to the next person? The story gets twisted almost immediately. *"Now the serpent was more cunning than any beast of the field which the Lord God had made. And he said to the woman, "Has God indeed said, 'You shall not eat of every tree of the garden'"* (Genesis 3:1)? Who is speaking through the serpent to the woman? Revelation 12:9 gives us a big clue: *"So the great dragon was cast out, that serpent of old, called the Devil and Satan, who deceives the whole world; he was cast to the earth, and his angels were cast out with him."* We will discuss in a later chapter more details about the origin and destiny of Satan, but for the purpose here, the speaking of the serpent was a diabolic miracle, just as the speaking of Balaam's donkey was a divine miracle (Numbers 22:28).

Note how Satan twisted God's word, casting doubt upon the woman. *"When he speaks a lie, he speaks from his own resources, for he is a liar and the father of it"* (John 8:44). God said they could eat from every tree (with one exception). Satan said to the woman, in effect, "Since God said to be fruitful and multiply, fill the earth and subdue it and have dominion over every living thing, how come you can't eat from any tree you want? Clearly you must have heard it wrong from your husband?" A marriage counselor Satan is not. Give him an inch in your life and he takes a foot. Now the woman starts to second-guess what her husband told her about the tree of knowledge.

The woman's response to the serpent in Genesis 3:2-3: *"We may eat the fruit of the trees of the garden; but of the fruit of the tree which is in the midst of the garden, God has said, 'You shall not eat it, nor shall you touch it, lest you die.'"* The translation from God to Adam, then from Adam to the woman (she had no formal name yet) and then add in Satan's distorted lies and you have a recipe for disaster. Where did God say, "You shall not touch the fruit of knowledge?" Even more importantly, where did God say, "You shall die immediately if you touch or eat the fruit of knowledge?" The woman's belief that if she even touched the tree's fruit, death was imminent, inferred that the conversation with the serpent took place well away from "the tree which is in the midst of the garden." In the original Hebrew language, the woman's interpretation of "die" in Genesis 3:3 meant immediate death, whereas God said in Genesis 2:17 that "you shall surely die," meaning the process of physically dying would begin, as witnessed in Adam's life, dying at the ripe age of 930 (Genesis 5:5).

It gets even more twisted. *"Then the serpent said to the woman, 'You will not surely die. For God knows that in the day you eat of it your eyes will be opened, and you will be like God, knowing good and evil'"* (Genesis 3:4-5). Satan responded by telling the woman, "You will not surely die," which was a lie but in her mind he meant she would not die immediately, which was cunningly true! Is it possible that Adam embellished God's instructions to the woman? Yes. He did have free will, but without the knowledge of good and evil. Is it possible that the woman misunderstood what Adam told her and/or added her own embellishments? Yes. She also had free will, but without the knowledge of good and evil. Again, I'm reminded of innocent children sitting in a circle of chairs whispering what has been said from one ear to the next. The story will not be the same come full circle. Whatever happened in the translation from God to the woman, it was done with innocence and without sin. But that strategic move by the serpent to tempt the woman first, thinking she was the weaker of the two, would ultimately be Satan's downfall when God imposes a curse.

Coveting someone or something that does not belong to you gives birth to sin. "*So when the woman saw that the tree was good for food, that it was pleasant to the eyes, and a tree desirable to make one wise, she took of its fruit and ate. She also gave to her husband with her, and he ate*" (Genesis 3:6). The woman "saw" with her "eyes," which built up an inward "desire," prompting her to "take" the fruit (meaning she touched it and did not die; the serpent must be telling the truth) and finally doing what God forbad – she "ate." At this point, sin still has not affected mankind but for one final and fatal step. Adam, who was with her, who was to "tend" and "keep" the garden and protect the woman from harm, failed! He consummated that failure when "he ate" also. Uh oh! "*Then the eyes of both of them were opened, and they knew that they were naked*" (Genesis 3:7). Temptation turned into sin and the pending curses on creation were born.

After the blame game takes place in Genesis 3:12-13 (man blames woman, woman blames serpent) of who said and did what, God lays down the hammer on creation – starting first with the serpent. *"Because you have done this, you are cursed more than all cattle, and more than every beast of the field; on your belly you shall go, and you shall eat dust all the days of your life"* (Genesis 3:14). The Hebrew root word for serpent translates to be a snake, which is now cursed to its belly. In addition, note how all cattle and every beast is also cursed with the snake. What is the curse? Death. "All the days of your life" means time is now ticking on the number of days left to live. The first recorded death was an animal sacrifice (innocent blood shed for atonement of sin) recorded in Genesis 3:21 where God made tunics of skin (in place of fig leaves in Genesis 3:7) to cover Adam and his wife. All life will "surely die" (physical death) because of sin and return to the dust of the earth. Deuteronomy 30:19-20 states, *"I call heaven and earth as witnesses today against you, that I have set before you life and death, blessing and cursing; therefore choose life, that both you and your descendants may live; that you may love the Lord your God, that you may obey His voice, and that you may cling to Him, for He is your life and the length of your days."* Unfortunately Adam and the woman disobeyed God, and in doing so, a physical death would become their curse also. But God had a backup plan for such disobedience.

The serpent was the agent of Satan and God's redemptive plan for mankind to be restored to Him in grace, truth and mercy was boldly stated in verse 15: "*And I will put enmity between you and the woman, and between your seed and her Seed; He shall bruise your head, and you shall bruise His heel.*" Enmity means hostility and hatred. Ask Satan whom he hates more – man or woman? Your answer is in Genesis 3:15. Satan would be defeated by what he perceived to be the weaker vessel – the woman (after all, she didn't even have a formal name when the conversation took place).

It would ultimately be a woman, a virgin named Mary (Matthew 1:18-25), who would bring forth the "Seed" conceived of the Holy Spirit in childbirth, the son of God, Jesus Christ. Satan would bruise His heel at the cross, but three days later Christ crushed Satan's head by conquering death, hell and the grave. "*Inasmuch then as the children have partaken of flesh and blood, He Himself likewise shared in the same, that through death He might destroy him who had the power of death, that is, the devil*" (Hebrews 2:14). The Garden Tomb in Jerusalem is the only attraction in the world where people will spend money to see nothing, for He has risen! Jesus said, "I have the keys of Hades and of Death" (Revelation 1:18). Satan's curse was the woman, who would give birth to the Son of God. Is there no wonder there is so much animosity toward women in the ministry? Every person should closely examine themselves (spiritual discernment) when it comes to such matters. *"For if anyone thinks himself to be something, when he is nothing, he deceives himself. But let each one examine his own work, and then he will have rejoicing in himself alone, and not in another. For each one shall bear his own load"* (Galatians 6:3-5). Suffice it to say women play a vital role in spreading the good news that Jesus Christ lives (Mark 16:9-11), becoming the firstfruits from the dead (1 Corinthians 15:20).

"To the woman He said: 'I will greatly multiply your sorrow and your conception; in pain you shall bring forth children; your desire shall be for your husband, and he shall rule over you'" (Genesis 3:16). The woman still has no name when the curse is laid out by God. She would be named later by Adam in Genesis 3:20 because she is the mother of all living. The sentence upon the woman deals with the two aspects of the married woman's life as wife and mother. The woman's biological system regarding ovulation, sex and conception would be cursed with sorrow and pain. No longer would childbearing be painless and full

of joy, having many children to multiply the earth, and living forever as God intended in His perfect creation. Imagine conceiving a child and the pregnancy produces a miscarriage or stillbirth. Imagine the sorrow Eve must have felt when the first murder (Genesis 4:8) happens between her two sons, Cain killing Abel. That is a curse!

Furthermore as a wife, the woman was created as man's equal. "*And the Lord God said, 'It is not good that man should be alone; I will make him a helper comparable to him'*" (Genesis 2:18). She was made to provide help, relief and aid to Adam. He was to tend and keep the garden, and she would be his relief, capable of performing the same task. "*Therefore a man shall leave his father and mother and be joined to his wife, and they shall become one flesh*" (Genesis 2:24). God ordained this first marriage between one man and one woman. As a wife, God in Genesis 3:16 also stated, "*Your desire shall be for your husband, and he shall rule over you.*" Because of Eve's disobedience to God and subsequent manipulation of her husband, her "desire" will now be for her husband's needs as he leads his family spiritually. Adam is now charged to be the head of the family. Of course, if the husband fails to lead his family in spiritual matters and love his wife as Christ loved the church (Ephesians 5:25), it leads to discourse and more sorrow for the woman. "*And you, fathers, do not provoke your children to wrath, but bring them up in the training and admonition of the Lord*" (Ephesians 6:4). God encourages equality in marriage when it comes to being one flesh. "*The wife does not have authority over her own body, but the husband does. And likewise the husband does not have authority over his own body, but the wife does*" (1 Corinthians 7:4). Spiritually, "wives, submit to your own husbands, as to the Lord" (Ephesians 5:22). So husband, if God is not first in your life, all bets are off when it comes to your wife submitting to your ungodly leadership. This is why God, the ultimate marriage counselor, implores us in 2 Corinthians 6:14: "*Do not be unequally yoked together with unbelievers.*" Unequally yoked literally means to have fellowship with one who is not an equal. Equality in marriage starts with both the husband and wife believing in Jesus Christ.

To all the environmentalists, this curse is for you. "*Then to Adam He said, 'Because you have heeded the voice of your wife, and have eaten from the tree of which I commanded you, saying, 'You shall not eat of it': 'Cursed is the ground for your sake; in toil you shall eat of it all the days of your life. Both thorns and thistles it shall bring forth for you, and you shall eat the herb of the field. In the sweat of your face you shall eat bread till you return to the ground, for out of it you were taken; for dust you are, and to dust you shall return"* (Genesis 3:17-19). The ground is cursed in two ways! No longer will there be a garden of Eden that produces boundless fruit, including fruit from the tree of life that provides immortality (Genesis 3:22), but now the ground will bring forth "thorns and thistles" that man must toil by the sweat of his brow just to produce food to eat. The second way the ground is cursed is by way of death ("all the days of your life"), which until sin entered the picture did not exist. The ground now becomes a graveyard for all mankind. *"It is appointed for men to die once, but after this the judgment"* (Hebrews 9:27). *"For as by one man's disobedience many were made sinners, so also by one Man's obedience many will be made righteous"* (Romans 5:19). *"For the wages of sin is death, but the gift of God is eternal life in Christ Jesus our Lord"* (Romans 6:23). God provided a way (Jesus) to reverse the death curse.

As for the earth itself, the ground is still under a curse of corruption. In essence, the ground is no longer holy and pure. Men normally wore sandals, and it was ceremonially important to wash the cursed soil off one's feet before entering a house (Genesis 18:4; 19:2; 43:24; Judges 19:21; Luke 7:44). Jesus set the ultimate example for feet washing in John 13. *"Then He came to Simon Peter. And Peter said to Him, 'Lord, are You washing my feet?' Jesus answered and said to him, 'What I am doing you do not understand now, but you will know after this.' Peter said to Him, 'You shall never wash my feet!' Jesus answered him, 'If I do not wash you, you have no part with Me.'"* (John 13:6-8). Strong words from the son of God. Why? Because the ground, specifically the dust, is cursed because of sin. Holy ground, where the curse was removed, required men to go barefoot. Just ask Moses at the burning bush on Mount Horeb when God spoke to him. *"Then He said, 'Do not draw near this place. Take your sandals off your feet, for the place where you stand is holy ground.'"* (Exodus 3:5). Joshua was commanded to remove his sandals due to holy ground (Joshua 5:15). Jewish custom required the priest on duty in the temple to be barefoot.

"Because the creation itself also will be delivered from the bondage of corruption into the glorious liberty of the children of God. For we know that the whole creation groans and labors with birth pangs together until now. Not only that, but we also who have the firstfruits of the Spirit, even we ourselves

groan within ourselves, eagerly waiting for the adoption, the redemption of our body" (Romans 8:21-23). God will reverse all curses on creation one glorious day. The earth and heavens will be resurrected from the "bondage of corruption" just as our bodies will be resurrected in the likeness of Jesus, if you have accepted Him as Lord and Savior (Romans 6:5). "*Nevertheless we, according to His promise, look for new heavens and a new earth in which righteousness dwells*" (2 Peter 3:13). There is nothing mankind can do to stop God from re-creating a new earth from the current cursed version we live on now!

Thorns, thistles and briers exist "*because of the ground which the Lord has cursed*" (Genesis 5:29). Jesus, the son of God, spoke of thorns in the parable of the sower (Matthew 13; Mark 4). He said that thorns choke good seed and render them unfruitful. That is what sin does to those who hear the word, but still desire worldly things (cares, riches and other unrighteous things). Sin literally chokes the life (specifically eternal life) from people who hear the Word of God and still ignore its message.

Thorns inflict physical pain. By comparison, sin inflicts emotional and spiritual pain. King David can attest to the agony in Psalm 25:18 as he pleads to God, "*Look on my affliction and my pain, and forgive all my sins."* Gideon used thorns with briers to tear the flesh of the leaders of Succoth for questioning him as God's servant (Judges 8:7, 16). In 2 Corinthians 12:7, Paul talked of "a thorn in the flesh was given to me, a messenger of Satan to buffet me." The word "buffet" means to strike with the fist, give one a blow with the fist, to maltreat or treat with violence. Note how Satan is associated with the thorn. Which brings me to the ultimate use of thorns to inflict pain, the twisted crown of thorns. *"When they had twisted a crown of thorns, they put it on His head, and a reed in His right hand. And they bowed the knee before Him and mocked Him, saying, 'Hail, King of the Jews!'"* (Matthew 27:29). Thorns, a curse on this earth because of sin and a tool used by Satan to inflict pain, was placed on the head of Jesus during His crucifixion. At the cross, God the Father placed the sins of the whole world (1 John 2:2) on His Son, Jesus, *"who Himself bore our sins in His own body on the tree, that we, having died to sins, might live for righteousness"* (1 Peter 2:24). The next time you feel a prick when you pick a lily among thorns (Song of Solomon 2:2) or smell a rose, think of the physical, emotional and spiritual pain Jesus went through bearing your sins as He wore a crown of thorns.

In the end, thorns are worthy of one thing – fire! And the source of that fire is God Himself, for He is a consuming fire (Exodus 24:17; Deuteronomy 4:24, 9:3; Hebrews 12:29). *"Now if anyone builds on this foundation with gold, silver, precious stones, wood, hay, straw, each one's work will become clear; for the Day will declare it, because it will be revealed by fire; and the fire will test each one's work, of what sort it is. If anyone's work which he has built on it endures, he will receive a reward. If anyone's work is burned, he will suffer loss; but he himself will be saved, yet so as through fire"* (1 Corinthians 3:12-15). I love this body of scripture. The "foundation" is Jesus Christ, the "gold, silver, precious stones" is your work done with pure motive as a Christian, the "wood, hay, straw" are works done with an impure motive (sin), and "revealed by fire" means every thought, word and deed will be tested by God Himself. I call it the sniff test! Good work is refined by fire, resulting in you getting "a reward." Bad work is consumed by fire and you "will suffer loss," for He is a consuming fire. This judgment of work takes place for Christians in heaven ("but he himself will be saved") after we physically die. The judgment for all your sins took place at the cross and were forgiven when you asked Jesus to be your Savior. But what about those who do not ask Jesus to be their Savior? Fire is their future.

The future destiny for all sin, represented by thorns, is fire. "*For the earth which drinks in the rain that often comes upon it, and bears herbs useful for those by whom it is cultivated, receives blessing from God; but if it bears thorns and briers, it is rejected and near to being cursed, whose end is to be burned*" (Hebrews 6:7-8). "*For wickedness burns as the fire; it shall devour the briers and thorns, and kindle in the thickets of the forest; they shall mount up like rising smoke*" (Isaiah 9:18). The lake of fire is the eternal home for Satan (Revelation 20:10), the beast and false prophet (Revelation 19:20), Death and Hades (Revelation 20:14), and anyone not found written in the Book of Life (Revelation 20:15), meaning the cowardly, unbelieving, abominable, murderers, sexually immoral, sorcerers, idolaters, and all liars (Revelation 21:8). The key word is "unbelieving" – those who rejected the sacrifice Jesus gave for their sins. They have to pay the death penalty themselves – TWICE! The lake of fire is the second death (Revelation 20:14). What are sins and thorns good for? Fire.

As this chapter concludes, the ultimate curse imposed by God on humanity for sin was death, hell and the grave. No longer in reach was the tree of life in the garden of Eden that produced immortality fruit (Genesis 3:22). "*Then the Lord God said, 'Behold, the man has become like one of Us, to know good and evil. And now, lest he put out his hand and take also of the tree of life, and eat, and live forever' — therefore the Lord God sent him out of the garden of Eden to till the ground from which he was taken. So He drove out the man; and He placed cherubim at the east of the garden of Eden, and a flaming sword which turned every way, to guard the way to the tree of life*" (Genesis 3:22-24). That tree of life still exist today. It produces twelve fruits, a different kind every month, and contains leaves to heal the nations (Revelation 22:2).

The good news is that Jesus is the way, truth and life (John 14:6). To punch your ticket to heaven and defeat this curse, accept His gift of eternal life by believing in Him as your Savior and He will give you a measure of faith (Romans 12:3) to continue in that belief. "*These things I have written to you who believe in the name of the Son of God, that you may know that you have eternal life, and that you may continue to believe in the name of the Son of God*" (1 John 5:13). "*To him who overcomes I will give to eat from the tree of life, which is in the midst of the Paradise of God*" (Revelation 2:7).

Chapter Four
Control

"*As you do not know what is the way of the wind, or how the bones grow in the womb of her who is with child, so you do not know the works of God who makes everything*" (Ecclesiastes 11:5). We have already established that our Creator (discussed in Chapter one) made everything you see and don't see in creation (in Chapter two). The curses discussed in previous chapters are still in effect, "*For we know that the whole creation groans and labors with birth pangs together until now*" (Romans 8:22). God is in control of it all. "*And He said to them, 'It is not for you to know times or seasons which the Father has put in His own authority'*" (Acts 1:7). And the Father gave that authority to His Son. "*And Jesus came and spoke to them, saying, 'All authority has been given to Me in heaven and on earth'*" (Matthew 28:18). Authority means power. Power to control all nature – in heaven and earth.

The only commands God gave man regarding the earth was to be fruitful and multiply (fill the earth), subdue it and have dominion over every living thing (Genesis 1:28). "*And the fear of you and the dread of you shall be on every beast of the earth, on every bird of the air, on all that move on the earth, and on all the fish of the sea. They are given into your hand*" (Genesis 9:2). Mankind is to tend and keep or bring into bondage the earth while ruling over all animal life that moves. It is called stewardship (specifically, the management, oversight, and administration of another's property). However, God maintains ownership of it all – including each breath you take. "*Thus says God the Lord, Who created the heavens and stretched them out, Who spread forth the earth and that which comes from it, Who gives breath to the people on it, and spirit to those who walk on it*" (Isaiah 42:5).

As of 2016, the topic "climate change" in Wikipedia had the following quote: "Certain human activities have also been identified as significant causes of recent climate change, often referred to as global warming." After reading this chapter, you will find this quote to be absurd on its face. Humans, who are a part of creation, can cause the climate to change? Wow! I had no idea we had the authority and power of God, the Creator, to control the temperature outside, prevent storms, earthquakes and seas from rising. This line of thought can lead to paganism, specifically the worshipping of creation (more on this later). If human activity of today can cause "climate change" (the first car with combustion engine was made in 1886), then one can conclude "climate change" did not exist from the time of Adam and Eve till 1885. That is a recorded span of about 5900 years! The only means of travel was by foot or animal prior to the early 1800s when modern bicycles were used. There were no cars, airplanes, factories, etc. supposedly polluting the air. Did "climate change" exist since the beginning of time? And if so, what human activity could have caused it? Let's dig deeper.

We don't have to read far in the Genesis account to see how God controls everything He created. *"So the Lord said, 'I will destroy man whom I have created from the face of the earth, both man and beast, creeping thing and birds of the air, for I am sorry that I have made them'"* (Genesis 6:7). Did God make a mistake? No. Man, having free will, continuously disobeyed God. *"Then the Lord saw that the wickedness of man was great in the earth, and that every intent of the thoughts of his heart was only evil continually. And the Lord was sorry that He had made man on the earth, and He was grieved in His heart"* (Genesis 6:5-6). The curse of sin ("wickedness") brought sadness to God, for "He was grieved in His heart." "*But Noah found grace in the eyes of the Lord*" (Genesis 6:8). If God made a mistake, He would have wiped out all of humanity.

"*The earth also was corrupt before God, and the earth was filled with violence. So God looked upon the earth, and indeed it was corrupt; for all flesh had corrupted their way on the earth*" (Genesis 6:11-12). Something had to be done by God to restore some order. A wicked, violent, corrupt earth would eventually consume Noah and his family. Satan was completely happy with this state of affairs because his goal was to prevent the Seed (Jesus) of the woman (Mary) from ever being born (Genesis 3:15). "*And behold, I Myself am bringing floodwaters on the earth, to destroy from under heaven all flesh in which is the breath of life; everything that is on the earth shall die*" (Genesis 6:17). Causing imminent death for every living thing on dry land is power. Only the ark was the way of escape. God saved Noah and his household (eight people) and the male and female of every living thing (Genesis 7:1–3). "*For after seven more days I will cause it to rain on the earth forty days and forty nights, and I will destroy from the face of the earth all living things that I have made*" (Genesis 7:4). God controls the rain and water levels.

"He who builds His layers in the sky, and has founded His strata in the earth; Who calls for the waters of the sea, and pours them out on the face of the earth— The Lord is His name" (Amos 9:6). Go back and review the six days of creation discussed in chapter two of this book when God separated the waters with a firmament, producing layers in the sky and water on the face of the earth (Genesis 1:6-8). *"When He assigned to the sea its limit, so that the waters would not transgress His command, when He marked out the foundations of the earth"* (Proverbs 8:29). On the third day of creation dry land appeared and God set borders for the seas, a command mankind has no effect on. *"He causes the vapors to ascend from the ends of the earth"* (Psalm 135:7). Water vapor is continuously generated by evaporation and removed by condensation. It is lighter than air and triggers convection currents that can lead to clouds. *"I set My rainbow in the cloud, and it shall be for the sign of the covenant between Me and the earth. It shall be, when I bring a cloud over the earth, that the rainbow shall be seen in the cloud"* (Genesis 9:13-14). Never again shall there be a flood to destroy the earth (Genesis 9:11). God controls the whole process to replenish the earth (vapor, clouds and rain). *"The*

43

Lord will open to you His good treasure, the heavens, to give the rain to your land in its season" (Deuteronomy 28:12).

"For He says to the snow, 'Fall on the earth'; likewise to the gentle rain and the heavy rain of His strength" (Job 37:6). "By the breath of God ice is given, and the broad waters are frozen" (Job 37:10). God controls when rain turns to snow, how heavy the rain falls, and where, when and how much of the water freezes. Mankind has no power regarding this natural yearly occurrence. It's called summer and winter. "You have set all the borders of the earth; You have made summer and winter" (Psalm 74:17). "To everything there is a season, a time for every purpose under heaven" (Ecclesiastes 3:1). "And He changes the times and the seasons" (Daniel 2:21).

What about storms? Can humans help prevent the severity of storms. No! "The Lord sent thunder and hail, and fire darted to the ground. And the Lord rained hail on the land of Egypt" (Exodus 9:23). God controls storms and how much wind, thunder, lightning and hail is produced. Hail forms in strong thunderstorm clouds, particularly those with intense updrafts, high liquid water content, great vertical extent, large water droplets, and where a good portion of the cloud layer is below freezing. These types of strong updrafts can also produce tornados. "*He casts out His hail like morsels ... He sends out His word and melts them*" (Psalm 147:17-18). As for the firework show in the sky darting to the ground, "*He makes lightning for the rain*" (Psalm 135:7). "*His lightnings light the world*" (Psalm 97:4).

God created the weather patterns. "*The wind goes toward the south, and turns around to the north; the wind whirls about continually, and comes again on its circuit*" (Ecclesiastes 1:6). Meteorologists study things in the air. In 350 B.C., Aristotle (considered the founder of meteorology) is credited in discovering the global wind patterns. Winds were named by the direction from which they blew. The earth is encircled by six major wind belts, three in each hemisphere. All six belts move north in the northern summer and south in the northern winter. One problem with this discovery. God already revealed the wind pattern in Ecclesiastes (read 1:6 again above) in approximately 935 B.C., approximately 585 years earlier.

God controls the wind. "*He brings the wind out of His treasuries*" (Psalm 135:7). "*He caused an east wind to blow in the heavens; and by His power He brought in the south wind*" (Psalm 78:26). God controls the direction of wind. "*And the Lord turned a very strong west wind*" (Exodus 10:19).

God controls how strong the wind is. "*The Lord brought an east wind on the land all that day and all that night*" (Exodus 10:13). God controls how long the wind blows. "*For He commands and raises the stormy wind, which lifts up the waves of the sea*" (Psalm 107:25). God controls the tropical cyclone (hurricane, typhoon, etc.), which grows in strength over the warm seas evaporation. "*But the Lord sent out a great wind on the sea, and there was a mighty tempest on the sea, so that the ship was about to be broken up*" (Jonah 1:4). God controls what the wind targets. "*Behold, a whirlwind of the Lord has gone forth in fury— A violent whirlwind!*" (Jeremiah 23:19). God controls the tornado. "*After these things I saw four angels standing at the four corners of the earth, holding the four winds of the earth, that the wind should not blow on the earth, on the sea, or on any tree*" (Revelation 7:1). God controls the wind to not blow. "*The Lord has His way in the whirlwind and in the storm, and the clouds are the dust of His feet*" (Nahum 1:3). God has a will and His way is the only way. Mankind has no influence whatsoever preventing the severity, direction or pattern of storms.

Since God has all authority and power when it comes to His creation, He can break the laws of nature. We call it supernatural power. Forty days and forty nights of rain is a supernatural event, never to happen again by the sign of His rainbow. Forty days of floodwaters covering the entire earth is supernatural. "And God made a wind to pass over the earth, and the waters subsided" (Genesis 8:1). A supernatural wind caused the waters to go back to their borders. *"But He said to them, 'Why are you fearful, O you of little faith?' Then He arose and rebuked the winds and the sea, and there was a great calm. So the men marveled, saying, 'Who can this be, that even the winds and the sea obey Him?'"* (Matthew 8:26-27). Jesus, the son of God, is His name. *"Now in the fourth watch of the night Jesus went to them, walking on the sea"* (Matthew 14:25). Jesus made water His sidewalk. It was a supernatural event when Jesus made water into wine (John 4:46). *"The Lord caused the sea to go back by a strong east wind all that night, and made the sea into dry land, and the waters were divided"* (Exodus 14:21). God used Moses to part the Red Sea. He used Joshua (Joshua 3:15-17), Elijah (2 Kings 2:7-8) and Elisha (2 Kings 2:13-14) to part the Jordan River on three occasions. In all four partings, they walked on dry land (as opposed to wet mud or sinking sand) while wind held the walls of water at bay by His command. And lest we forget the supernatural event of creation itself when the waters (in one day) were divided by a firmament

47

to form the sky.

What about the earth? *"Then the earth shook and trembled; the foundations of the hills also quaked and were shaken, because He was angry"* (Psalm 18:7). God controls earthquakes. *"Then the earth shook and trembled; the foundations of heaven quaked and were shaken, because He was angry"* (2 Samuel 22:8). God controls the severity of earthquakes. *"Behold, the Lord makes the earth empty and makes it waste, distorts its surface and scatters abroad its inhabitants"* (Isaiah 24:1). God can rearrange His creation when and how He wants to accomplish His will. *"Come, behold the works of the Lord, Who has made desolations in the earth"* (Psalm 46:8). God controls where life grows. *"He causes the grass to grow for the cattle, and vegetation for the service of man, that he may bring forth food from the earth"* (Psalm 104:14). God controls where food will grow. *"The earth shall answer with grain, with new wine, and with oil"* (Hosea 2:22). God controls where grain, wine and oil is produced on earth. Oil is a natural source for energy and it comes from God. I guess environmentalists would say God polluted the earth.

So why does a good God (Psalm 136:1) allow natural disasters to deface His creation, including killing humans in some cases? If you recall, creation was perfectly made and God saw that everything was very good, not just good (Genesis 1:31). Sin entered the world through the fall of Adam and Eve, resulting in the curse of thorns and thistles on His creation and a physical death to all living things. Sin has consequences! *"For the creation was subjected to futility, not willingly, but because of Him who subjected it in hope"* (Romans 8:20). Futility means devoid of truth, perverseness and depravity. Nature and the animal kingdom were forced into corruption and bondage by the free will of man to disobey God. The end result? The earth, awaiting a new birth, groans in agony and pain as a consequence of man's sin (Romans 8:22). However, Jesus is the truth and all of creation's hope because everything seen and unseen was made by, for and through Him. *"Behold, now is the accepted time; behold, now is the day of salvation"* (2 Corinthians 6:2). This is why it is important to accept salvation from the Lord today, even more urgent than that … now! We are not guaranteed our next breath. We are guaranteed to be in His presence upon death if we accept Jesus as Savior. *"So we are always confident, knowing that while we are at home in the body we are absent from the Lord. For we walk by faith, not by sight. We are confident, yes, well pleased rather to be absent from the body and to be present with the Lord"* (2 Corinthians 5:6-

8). It's not by coincidence that the great commission follows Jesus' declarative statement of all power, control and authority given to Him. *"All authority has been given to Me in heaven and on earth. Go therefore and make disciples of all the nations, baptizing them in the name of the Father and of the Son and of the Holy Spirit"* (Matthew 28:18-19).

What about the constellations? *"Thus says the Lord, Who gives the sun for a light by day, the ordinances of the moon and the stars for a light by night"* (Jeremiah 31:35). Everything God controls gives. The sun gives light. The moon and stars do the same. Rain gives nourishment for grass, plants, trees and food. God the Father gave His Son. Jesus gave His life for us. His sacrificial blood gives those who believe eternal life. *"Those by the wayside are the ones who hear; then the devil comes and takes away the word out of their hearts, lest they should believe and be saved"* (Luke 8:12). By contrast, Satan is a taker. *"The day is Yours, the night also is Yours; You have prepared the light and the sun"* (Psalm 74:16). *"He appointed the moon for seasons; the sun knows its going down"* (Psalm 104:19). God controls the sun and moon. There is nothing mankind can do to prevent the intensity of the sun's energy or where and when it shines its light on earth.

To drive the point home about absolute control, authority and power over His creation, God can supernaturally alter celestial objects – the earth and heavens. *"So the sun stood still, and the moon stopped ... So the sun stood still in the midst of heaven, and did not hasten to go down for about a whole day"* (Joshua 10:13). God can stop time since He is the author of time. In this case God even gives us a clue that the earth rotates on an axis and around the sun ("the sun stood still") and the moon rotates around the earth ("the moon stopped"). If the sun moved around the earth, it would also need to be stopped. Nicolaus Copernicus has been credited in discovering that the earth orbits the sun in the 16th century. The Book of Joshua was approximately written between 1400 and 1370 B.C. It took someone close to 3000 years after the above inspired scripture is penned to put two and two together. During battle, Joshua prayed to the Lord for the sun and moon to stop, so he would have extra daylight to finish the task. The result was time (earth and moon) stood still for hours. *"The sun and moon stood still in their habitation"* (Habakkuk 3:11).

Not only can God stop time, He can also reverse it. *"So Isaiah the prophet cried out to the Lord, and He brought the shadow ten degrees backward*" (2 Kings 20:11). King Hezekiah was sick and near death when he tearfully prayed to the Lord (2 Kings 20:1-3). God's response via the prophet Isaiah was to heal Hezekiah and add fifteen more years to his life (2 Kings 20:4-6). God controls every breath you take! Not just taking Isaiah's word for it, Hezekiah wanted a sign from God he would be healed (2 Kings 20:8). "*So the sun returned ten degrees on the dial by which it had gone down*" (Isaiah 38:8). God caused the earth to rotate backwards on its axis and orbit around the sun in reverse for approximately 40 minutes. Imagine sunset, dusk is upon you, and the sun disappears over the horizon only to come back up and shine its light upon you for another 40 minutes. "*He commands the sun, and it does not rise; He seals off the stars*" (Job 9:7). That is a sign. That is control!

What about animals and all living creatures? "*Out of the ground the Lord God formed every beast of the field and every bird of the air, and brought them to Adam to see what he would call them. And whatever Adam called each living creature, that was its name*" (Genesis 2:19). "*Of the birds after their kind, of animals after their kind, and of every creeping thing of the earth after its kind, two of every kind will come to you to keep them alive*" (Genesis 6:20). God controls all living things that breathe, even making them come to Adam (to be named) and Noah (to be saved). "*And the fear of you and the dread of you shall be on every beast of the earth, on every bird of the air, on all that move on the earth, and on all the fish of the sea. They are given into your hand. Every moving thing that lives shall be food for you. I have given you all things, even as the green herbs. But you shall not eat flesh with its life, that is, its blood*" (Genesis 9:2). After the floodwaters, meat now became part of the human diet. God gave every beast "dread," the instinct to flee mankind.

The following slogan comes from PETA (People for the Ethical Treatment of Animals): "Animals are not ours to eat, wear, experiment on, use for entertainment, or abuse in any other way." God sacrificed an animal (if I had to guess, likely a lamb) in the garden of Eden, spilling innocent blood to atone for man's sin and then covering their nakedness with the animal skin. After the flood, God said to Noah we can eat animals as we do green herbs. PETA's slogan regarding food and clothing is contrary to God's Word. They are correct in their stance that animals are innocent. God is well aware of that fact. In the Old Testament, an innocent animal (blood sacrifice) had to die to atone for the sins of the guilty. Jesus Christ, the innocent Lamb of

God, ushered in the New Testament by fulfilling the same sin requirement once and for all at His crucifixion (Hebrews 7:26-27). *"But if we walk in the light as He is in the light, we have fellowship with one another, and the blood of Jesus Christ His Son cleanses us from all sin"* (1 John 1:7). The One who did no wrong died for your sins and my sins so that we may have eternal life through Him and be restored to a right relationship with God the Father. With that said, *"a righteous man regards the life of his animal"* (Proverbs 12:10). *"If you meet your enemy's ox or his donkey going astray, you shall surely bring it back to him again"* (Exodus 23:4). We are to be good stewards of all creation (where PETA is spot on regarding animal abuse), but make no mistake, God never gave up His ownership or control of His handiwork spoken into existence and formed from His dirt.

During the ten plagues God sent upon Egypt through Moses to convince Pharaoh to free the Israelite slaves from bondage and oppression endured for 400 years, God used and controlled even the tiniest of creatures. Why? Because Egypt worshipped creation (in many forms) rather than the one true God and Creator. *"So the river shall bring forth frogs abundantly, which shall go up and come into your house, into your bedroom, on your bed, into the houses of your servants, on your people, into your ovens, and into your kneading bowls*" (Exodus 8:3). In the second plague, frogs did the will of God and then died for the cause at God's command to send a stench in the land. The third plague brought forth lice, a wingless insect, from the dust of the ground upon man and beast in the land (Exodus 8:16-18). Pharaoh hardened his heart even more toward the Creator, so God sent swarms of flies (fourth plague) to pester only the Egyptians in their homes and land while not one fly bothered the Israelites (Exodus 8:20-24). And for the ultimate display of control, God used the curse of death for the fifth plague. "*Behold, the hand of the Lord will be on your cattle in the field, on the horses, on the donkeys, on the camels, on the oxen, and on the sheep—a very severe pestilence*" (Exodus 9:3). Yet God spared all the livestock of the Israelites (Exodus 9:4) while appointing the exact time the Egyptian livestock would die (Exodus 9:5).

As mentioned before in a previous chapter, God caused Balaam's donkey to speak (Numbers 22:28-30). That is a sad day when your donkey has more spiritual discernment than you do. God directed two milk cows to pull a cart containing the ark of the Lord back to Israel while the Philistines gave chase to no avail (I Samuel 6:10-12). The cows were then sacrificed as a burnt offering to the Lord using the wood from the cart. God commanded ravens to feed Elijah bread and meat (I Kings 17:2-6). God sent two female bears to kill forty-two youths for mocking Elisha (II Kings 2:23-24). Don't mock God's man by calling him baldheaded, even if he is. God shut the hungry lions' mouths when Daniel was thrown into the den, using them to stay warm through the night (Daniel 6:22). Then God unleashed their fury on Daniel's accusers, breaking every bone as they were devoured (Daniel 6:24). Again, don't mess with God's man. God prepared a great fish to swallow Jonah and then compelled it to vomit him on dry land after three whole days (Jonah 1:17; 2:10). Jesus, the son of God, caused a fish to bring Peter a coin so both could pay the temple tax (Matthew 17:27). All of the above represents total control, authority and power over all living things – from the smallest insect to the large serpent of the sea, the reptile Leviathan (Isaiah 27:1). Humans, on the other hand, have free will.

So with all that you have read above, who do you worship – creation or the Creator? If you worship creation, in any form, you are practicing paganism and committing idolatry. *"You shall have no other gods before Me"* (Exodus 20:3). The Earth Religion Anti-Abuse Resolution (1988) was written by the Church of All Worlds and affirmed by the Pagan Ecumenical Conferences of Ancient Ways (California, May 27–30) and Pagan Spirit Gathering (Wisconsin, June 17). The Pagan Community Council of Ohio then presented it to the Northeast Council of Wicca (Pagan Witchcraft). Here is the resolution in full: "We, the undersigned, as adherents of Pagan and Old and Neo-Pagan Earth Religions, including Wicca or Witchcraft, practice a variety of positive, life affirming faiths that are dedicated to healing, both of ourselves and of the Earth. As such, we do not advocate or condone any acts that victimize others, including those proscribed by law. As one of our most widely accepted precepts is the Wiccan Rede's injunction to 'harm none,' we absolutely condemn the practices of child abuse, sexual abuse and any other form of abuse that does harm to the bodies, minds or spirits of the victims of such abuses. We recognize and revere the divinity of Nature in our Mother the Earth, and we conduct our rites of worship in a manner that is ethical, compassionate and constitutionally protected. We neither acknowledge or worship the Christian devil, 'Satan,' who is not in our Pagan pantheons. We will not tolerate slander or libel against our Temples, clergy or Temple

Assemblers and we are prepared to defend our civil rights with such legal action as we deem necessary and appropriate."

It is fascinating in the resolution above that in describing nature they use the word "divinity." That would mean nature is in a state or quality of being divine, having the form of godliness, deity, and holiness. At the same time it rebukes the existence of a Creator, the divinity of Jesus Christ and spits in the face of God the Father by using the term "Mother the Earth." They even find it necessary to mention the non-existence of Satan because it would mean that the Bible, God's Word, is true. Their stance regarding nature is hardcore paganism, a religion that has many gods or goddesses, considers the earth holy, and does not have a central authority.

In contrast, let's look at what God said about worshipping nature. *"For since the creation of the world His invisible attributes are clearly seen, being understood by the things that are made, even His eternal power and Godhead, so that they are without excuse, because, although they knew God, they did not glorify Him as God, nor were thankful, but became futile in their thoughts, and their foolish hearts were darkened. Professing to be wise, they became fools, and changed the glory of the incorruptible God into an image made like corruptible man—and birds and four-footed animals and creeping things. Therefore God also gave them up to uncleanness, in the lusts of their hearts, to dishonor their bodies among themselves, who exchanged the truth of God for the lie, and worshiped and served the creature rather than the Creator, who is blessed forever*" (Romans 1:20-25). Our Creator has Godhead eternal power, meaning all divine authority and control belong to Him and Him alone. If you worship a creature, nature or creation in any form, you have exchanged the truth for a lie. And who is the father of lies? The answer is Satan (John 8:44). "*I will stretch out My hand against Judah, and against all the inhabitants of Jerusalem. I will cut off every trace of Baal from this place, the names of the idolatrous priests with the pagan priests*" (Zephaniah 1:4). God hates idolatry and paganism. "*Thus I cleansed them of everything pagan*" (Nehemiah 13:30).

"*You shall not make for yourself a carved image—any likeness of anything that is in heaven above, or that is in the earth beneath, or that is in the water under the earth; you shall not bow down to them nor serve them*" (Exodus 20:4-5). God warned us about idolatry in his second commandment given through Moses on Mount Sinai. "*Then he removed the idolatrous priests whom the kings of Judah had ordained to burn incense on the high places* in the cities of Judah and in the places all around Jerusalem, and those who burned incense to Baal, to the sun, to the moon, to the constellations, and to all the host of heaven" (2 Kings 23:5). In the days of kings, King Josiah restored true worship to the one true God and Creator in the temple by removing all the graven images (burning them to ashes), the pagan priests (executing them), and the ritual booths where sodomy and prostitution were rampant. "*Therefore, my beloved, flee from idolatry*" (1 Corinthians 10:14).

Lastly, God should always receive the glory and worship. "*Fear God and give glory to Him, for the hour of His judgment has come; and worship Him who made heaven and earth, the sea and springs of water*" (Revelation 14:7). Anything less is sin. "*Adulterers and adulteresses! Do you not know that friendship with the world is enmity with God? Whoever therefore wants to be a friend of the world makes himself an enemy of God*" (James 4:4). Ouch! That is some strong language but it has to be to bring our attention to what really matters. "*For what profit is it to a man if he gains the whole world, and loses his own soul*" (Matthew 16:26)? "*Do not love the world or the things in the world. If anyone loves the world, the love of the Father is not in him*" (1 John 2:15). "*Set your mind on things above, not on things on the earth*" (Colossians 3:2). Your very soul is at stake if you worship creation instead of the Creator.

Chapter Five
Change

I know that "climate change" is real because God set the laws of His creation in motion. *"While the earth remains, seedtime and harvest, cold and heat, winter and summer, and day and night shall not cease"* (Genesis 8:22). That's change but there is also a subtle, yet important clue in the phrase "while the earth remains." There will come a day when this cursed earth will no longer remain and there is absolutely nothing man can do to stop it. *"You, Lord, in the beginning laid the foundation of the earth, and the heavens are the work of Your hands. They will perish, but You remain; and they will all grow old like a garment; like a cloak You will fold them up, and they will be changed. But You are the same, and Your years will not fail"* (Hebrews 1:10-12). Creation will be changed by the unchangeable Creator (meaning His righteous character dealing with sin never changes). *"For I am the Lord, I do not change"* (Malachi 3:6). For the earth and the heavens, "they will be changed" is translated from the Greek to mean exchange one thing for another or to transform. The cursed creation will one day be transformed into a perfect paradise again, but this time without sin to corrupt it (Revelation 21:27; 22:3). The glorious innocent Lamb of God, the reason why everything exists, will be its light forever (Revelation 21:23; 22:5). *"Jesus Christ is the same yesterday, today, and forever"* (Hebrews 13:8).

I also know that "global warming" is destined for this earth, but it will be God-made, not man-made. As stated previously, God is a consuming fire (Exodus 24:17; Deuteronomy 4:24, 9:3; Hebrews 12:29). The last chapter of this book will go into detail about how Jesus has the final say-so regarding all of creation … and it involves fire for believers and unbelievers. This chapter explores God's weapon of choice against sin – fire! God-made global warming is coming. God has used fire in the past and will use it in the future. As Jesus so eloquently said in Luke 12:49, *"I came to send fire on the earth, and how I wish it were already kindled!"* *"Do you suppose that I came to give peace on earth? I tell you, not at all, but rather division."* (Luke 12:51). Jesus Christ is no pacifist. A pacifist would not make a grand entrance into Jerusalem during Passover (when multitudes come to the temple), turn tables and seats over, drive out the money changers and call them thieves (Matthew 21:11-13). Sin must be dealt with one way (John 14:6) or another. The other way described below is not a pretty picture for unbelievers.

"Who makes His angels spirits, His ministers a flame of fire" (Psalm 104:4)? Supernatural fire is God's ultimate display of His power to control His creation. In its natural state, fire is the exothermic chemical process of combustion, which then releases heat, light, and various reaction products. In other words, fire burns and occurs in nature by lightning strikes and volcanic activity. One of the products released by fire into the atmosphere is carbon dioxide (CO_2). *"And the Angel of the Lord appeared to him in a flame of fire from the midst of a bush. So he looked, and behold, the bush was burning with fire, but the bush was not consumed"* (Exodus 3:2). Moses witnessed supernatural fire with his own eyes in the burning bush that never burned on Mount Horeb. In Judges 6:21, the Angel of the Lord caused fire to come forth from a rock to consume the meat and unleavened bread. By contrast, imagine a fire so intense it consumes stones. *"Then the fire of the Lord fell and consumed the burnt sacrifice, and the wood and the stones and the dust, and it licked up the water that was in the trench"* (1 Kings 18:38).

In chapter three of Daniel, King Nebuchadnezzar of Babylon commanded mighty men of valor to bind Shadrach, Meshach, and Abed-Nego, and cast them into the burning fiery furnace (heated seven times more than usual). For what reason? They refused to worship Nebuchadnezzar, his gods or the golden image. What happened next is how God controls the effects of fire on the wicked and righteous at the same time. For the wicked, "*the flame of the fire killed those men who took up Shadrach, Meshach, and Abed-Nego*" (Daniel 3:22). For the righteous, "*they saw these men on whose bodies the fire had no power; the hair of their head was not singed nor were their garments affected, and the smell of fire was not on them*" (Daniel 3:27). God Himself protected them supernaturally through the same fire that killed the men who put them in the furnace! Another awesome display of controlling the natural effects of fire was when the prophet Elijah was taken up by a whirlwind into heaven in a chariot of fire with horses of fire (2 Kings 2:11). Material, horses and a human were protected from fire.

Brimstone is burning sulfur. On earth, elemental sulfur can be found near hot springs and volcanic regions in many parts of the world. Hydrogen sulfide is as toxic as hydrogen cyanide and kills by the inhibition of the respiratory system. Sulfur is also present in many types of meteorites. *"Upon the wicked He will rain coals; fire and brimstone and a burning wind shall be the portion of their cup"* (Psalm 11:6). Coals translates to be snares, meaning there is no escape from God's wrath. The burning wind comes from the brimstone, specifically the hydrogen sulfide gas released in the air. So if the fire and/or stones don't kill the wicked, the lack of oxygen will. *"The men of Sodom were exceedingly wicked and sinful against the Lord"* (Genesis 13:13). Sodom and Gomorrah set the standard on how God judges the righteous and wicked. Abraham asked the Lord a very important question in Genesis 18:23-25 concerning the city of Sodom: *"Would You also destroy the righteous with the wicked? Suppose there were fifty righteous within the city; would You also destroy the place and not spare it for the fifty righteous that were in it? Far be it from You to do such a thing as this, to slay the righteous with the wicked, so that the righteous should be as the wicked; far be it from You! Shall not the Judge of all the earth do right?"* Great question!

God's answer to Abraham was that He would not destroy Sodom for the sake of fifty, forty-five, forty, thirty, twenty or ten righteous people (Genesis 18:26-32). Abraham finally got the message that God would not destroy the righteous with the wicked, even if was just one person, namely his nephew, Lot. This is important to remember when it comes to the "end times" and God's wrath is poured out on the wicked via the twenty-one plagues unveiled in the Book of Revelation. God sent two angels (disguised as normal men) to Sodom for one purpose! Extract the righteous from the city of Sodom. *"When the morning dawned, the angels urged Lot to hurry, saying, 'Arise, take your wife and your two daughters who are here, lest you be consumed in the punishment of the city.' And while he lingered, the men took hold of his hand, his wife's hand, and the hands of his two daughters, the Lord being merciful to him, and they brought him out and set him outside the city"* (Genesis 19:15-16). God's angels forcibly removed Lot, his wife and daughters from the city. *"Then the Lord rained brimstone and fire on Sodom and Gomorrah, from the Lord out of the heavens"* (Genesis 19:24).

The before and after landscape is striking. *"And Lot lifted his eyes and saw all the plain of Jordan, that it was well watered everywhere (before the Lord destroyed Sodom and Gomorrah) like the garden of the Lord, like the land of Egypt as you go toward Zoar"* (Genesis 13:10). Imagine a land so rich in resources that it was compared to the garden of Eden. *"The whole land is brimstone, salt, and burning; it is not sown, nor does it bear, nor does any grass grow there, like the overthrow of Sodom and Gomorrah, Admah, and Zeboiim, which the Lord overthrew in His anger and His wrath"* (Deuteronomy 29:23). God so decimated Sodom and Gomorrah, archeologists have had difficulty finding the ruins. Sin has consequences, with fire and brimstone being the means of torment forever (Revelation 20:10, 14-15).

Going back to the covenant God made with creation after the worldwide flood, let's break down what He said in Genesis 8:21. God said in His heart, *"I will never again curse the ground for man's sake, although the imagination of man's heart is evil from his youth; nor will I again destroy every living thing as I have done."* Curse, as translated from Hebrew in this case, means any future floods would be abated, smaller or less intense. In other words, God promised (His rainbow in the cloud being the sign of covenant) to never have a worldwide flood. Because of man's sin, the curse of thorns and thistles on earth in Genesis 3:18 remains. Humanity would continue to do evil, even from youth. Secondly, God also promised to never kill every living thing on dry land. This covenant with creation is important to understand in the body of the scripture in chapter three of 2 Peter. *"For this they willfully forget: that by the word of God the heavens were of old, and the earth standing out of water and in the water, by which the world that then existed perished, being flooded with water. But the heavens and the earth which are now preserved by the same word, are reserved for fire until the day of judgment and perdition of ungodly men"* (2 Peter 3:5-7). God has reserved His creation, currently in bondage to sin, for fire. The ungodly is judged with utter destruction. This fire is not for the righteous, just as Lot was spared from the fire and brimstone in Sodom! *"A fire goes before Him, and burns up His enemies round about"* (Psalm 97:3). The children of God (1 John 3:1), having obtained salvation through Jesus (1 Thessalonians 5:9), are not His enemies.

"But, beloved, do not forget this one thing, that with the Lord one day is as a thousand years, and a thousand years as one day. The Lord is not slack concerning His promise, as some count slackness, but is longsuffering toward us, not willing that any should perish but that all should come to repentance" (2 Peter 3:8-9). Resurrections are the bookends for the thousand year reign of Christ on earth. To the Lord that thousand years is as a day ... His day! The first resurrection (in several waves) is for believers and takes place before He comes

back. The second resurrection takes place for unbelievers at the end of His reign, when time ends and eternity begins. More on this in the last chapter. *"But the day of the Lord will come as a thief in the night, in which the heavens will pass away with a great noise, and the elements will melt with fervent heat; both the earth and the works that are in it will be burned up. Therefore, since all these things will be dissolved, what manner of persons ought you to be in holy conduct and godliness, looking for and hastening the coming of the day of God, because of which the heavens will be dissolved, being on fire, and the elements will melt with fervent heat"* (2 Peter 3:10-12)? Remember, God promised after the flood that He would never again destroy every living thing. So how is the fire mentioned in 2 Peter 3 going to be used?

To all who are looking for global warming, the Book of Revelation unveils it in detail. This cleansing of the currently cursed earth is for one purpose; preparing for the coming thousand year reign of Christ while Satan is bound (Revelation 20:1-2). *"For wickedness burns as the fire; it shall devour the briers and thorns, and kindle in the thickets of the forest; they shall mount up like rising smoke. Through the wrath of the Lord of hosts the land is burned up, and the people shall be as fuel for the fire; no man shall spare his brother"* (Isaiah

9:18-19). The crown of thorns He wore on the cross (representing the wicked sins of the world) has been traded in for many righteous crowns at His second coming (Revelation 19:12). "*For behold, the Lord will come with fire and with His chariots, like a whirlwind, to render His anger with fury, and His rebuke with flames of fire. For by fire and by His sword the Lord will judge all flesh; and the slain of the Lord shall be many*" (Isaiah 66:15-16). Why leave some of the wicked alive? Because He promised He would. "*Therefore the curse has devoured the earth, and those who dwell in it are desolate. Therefore the inhabitants of the earth are burned, and few men are left*" (Isaiah 24:6). Ultimately, all the wicked will die and be reserved for final judgment at the second resurrection and death.

It should also be pointed out that after the rapture of the church (believers) to heaven, the nation of Israel (Jewish people) will be left on earth surrounded by the ungodly. No nation will come to their rescue and Israel will desperately seek peace through whatever means. For those who have heard the gospel and rejected Jesus Christ, God the Father will now give them the antichrist. The world will be looking for answers and the antichrist will broker peace with the nation of Israel. I imagine part of the peace deal will be to remove all the walls and gates in exchange to rebuild the temple. He will be so convincing that Israel will indeed bring down their walls of protection (Ezekiel 38:11). Satan will eventually lead a hoard of armies from several countries to attack and destroy the nation of Israel. But not to worry, because there is a spy in the sky. *"And I will bring him to judgment with pestilence and bloodshed; I will rain down on him, on his troops, and on the many peoples who are with him, flooding rain, great hailstones, fire, and brimstone"* (Ezekiel 38:22).

The same supernatural fire that kills the wicked will preserve God's chosen people. *"But now, thus says the Lord, who created you, O Jacob, and He who formed you, O Israel: 'Fear not, for I have redeemed you; I have called you by your name; You are Mine. When you pass through the waters, I will be with you; and through the rivers, they shall not overflow you. When you walk through the fire, you shall not be burned, nor shall the flame scorch you. For I am the Lord your God, The Holy One of Israel, your Savior'"* (Isaiah 43:1-3). From there God-made global warming kicks into high gear! The seventh seal is opened in heaven and there is complete silence for about half an hour (Revelation 8:1). God's awesome display of judgment and wrath is about to be unleashed on the wicked. It will be so intense that people will give new meaning to the phrase OMG! "Oh my God" will be spoken in angst and wonder while begging for mercy.

Angels are given the seven trumpets and another angel starts the "destroy by fire" process. *"Then the angel took the censer, filled it with fire from the altar, and threw it to the earth. And there were noises, thunderings, lightnings, and an earthquake"* (Revelation 8:5). *"The first angel sounded: And hail and fire followed, mingled with blood, and they were thrown to the earth. And a third of the trees were burned up, and all green grass was burned up"* (Revelation 8:7). The thorns, thistles and briers (caused by sin's curse) are consumed. The result of this cleansing will be new growth during the reign of Christ and His saints. *"Then the second angel sounded: And something like a great mountain burning with fire was thrown into the sea, and a third of the sea became blood"* (Revelation 8:8). The seas were spared from destruction in the great flood, but they will not escape the wrath of fire. The sixth trumpet releases the four angels bound at the great river Euphrates for the sole purpose of killing a third of mankind. *"And thus I saw the horses in the vision: those who sat on them had breastplates of fiery red, hyacinth blue, and sulfur yellow; and the heads of the horses were like the heads of lions; and out of their mouths came fire, smoke, and brimstone. By these three plagues a third of mankind was killed—by the fire and the smoke and the brimstone which came out of their mouths"* (Revelation 9:17-18). Yikes! A third of the trees, seas and wicked humanity destroyed.

Now God's angel dispatches two witnesses to earth. *"And if anyone wants to harm them, fire proceeds from their mouth and devours their enemies. And if anyone wants to harm them, he must be killed in this manner"* (Revelation 11:5). How must they be killed? By fire! God's two witnesses will prophesy and give their testimony for one thousand two hundred and sixty days. They will have power to stop rain, turn waters to blood, and strike the earth with all plagues, as often as they desire (Revelation 11:6). People will hate them and rejoice when the beast from the bottomless pit kills them. They are so hated their bodies are left in the streets for all to see. But God raises them from the dead after three-and-half days. *"And they ascended to heaven in a cloud, and their enemies saw them"* (Revelation 11:12). Clearly the two witnesses and their testimony is rejected by many.

Now comes a theological debate for the ages. Is there anyone left on earth after the rapture takes place who is still counted among the righteous or can still be saved through the blood of Jesus? The first resurrection takes place in various stages. Jesus, being the firstfruits of those who have died (1 Corinthians 15:20), paved the way for the resurrection of all who believe in Him. This may come as a shock to some, but the first wave of the first resurrection has already taken place. *"And the graves were opened; and many bodies of the saints who had fallen asleep were raised; and coming out of the graves after His resurrection, they went into the holy city and appeared to many"* (Matthew 27:52-53). We are currently waiting for the second wave of the first resurrection. *"For the Lord Himself will descend from heaven with a shout, with the voice of an archangel, and with the trumpet of God. And the dead in Christ will rise first. Then we who are alive and remain shall be caught up together with them in the clouds to meet the Lord in the air. And thus we shall always be with the Lord"* (1 Thessalonians 4:16-17). But even after the second wave (rapture), there will be a third wave. *"Then I saw the souls of those who had been beheaded for their witness to Jesus and for the word of God, who had not worshiped the beast or his image, and had not received his mark on their foreheads or on their hands. And they lived and reigned with Christ for a thousand years"* (Revelation 20:4).

Time is so precious and critical at this point that God commissions an angel to spread the gospel instead of relying on mankind via the Holy Spirit. The second coming of Christ on earth is at hand. *"Then I saw another angel flying in the midst of heaven, having the everlasting gospel to preach to those who dwell on the earth — to every nation, tribe, tongue, and people"* (Revelation 14:6). As promised, everyone will be exposed to the gospel at least once to either accept or reject Jesus. Our Creator never wants anyone to perish. Nowhere in scripture does God say the second wave of the first resurrection is delayed until everyone hears the gospel. What does that mean? The rapture could take place right now! Bear in mind that the same supernatural fire that destroys the unrighteous (those who have rejected Christ before the rapture) will not harm His chosen people, the nation of Israel (Daniel 3:27; Isaiah 43:2), or those who accept Jesus (Romans 1:18; Romans 5:9; 1 Thessalonians 5:9) from the angel's testimony in Revelation 14:6. However, according to Revelation 20:4 they may be beheaded by Satan's agents of evil for their witness to Jesus and for the word of God. *"Here is the patience of the saints; here are those who keep the commandments of God and the faith of Jesus. Then I heard a voice from heaven saying to me,*

'Write: 'Blessed are the dead who die in the Lord from now on'" (Revelation 14:12-13). "From now on" means after the rapture, but before the second coming of Jesus as KING OF KINGS, AND LORD OF LORDS (Revelation 19:11-16).

Our Creator of creation now gives everyone an urgent message! *"Then a third angel followed them, saying with a loud voice, 'If anyone worships the beast and his image, and receives his mark on his forehead or on his hand, he himself shall also drink of the wine of the wrath of God, which is poured out full strength into the cup of His indignation. He shall be tormented with fire and brimstone in the presence of the holy angels and in the presence of the Lamb. And the smoke of their torment ascends forever and ever; and they have no rest day or night, who worship the beast and his image, and whoever receives the mark of his name'"* (Revelation 14:9-11). This is God's 911 warning (see scripture verse numbers) to all unbelievers and it describes the second death, otherwise known as the lake of fire.

The "separation from God" doctrine has completely infiltrated many churches today and is a false teaching. *"The eyes of the Lord are in every place, keeping watch on the evil and the good"* (Proverbs 15:3). God is omnipresent. *"If I ascend into heaven, You are there; if I make my bed in hell, behold, You are there"* (Psalm 139:8). Read this carefully again: "*He shall be tormented with fire and brimstone in the presence of the holy angels and in the presence of the Lamb.*" Unbelievers want nothing to do with God! As a matter of fact, they would love nothing more than to be separated from God. In Hades they are not separated. When they are cast into eternal hell (the lake of fire), they will not be separated from God. "*In flaming fire taking vengeance on those who do not know God, and on those who do not obey the gospel of our Lord Jesus Christ. These shall be punished with everlasting destruction from the presence of the Lord and from the glory of His power*" (2 Thessalonians 1:8-9). The everlasting destruction comes from the presence, glory and power of the Lord! Unbelievers will spend eternity in the presence of the Lamb of God, whom they rejected, and experience the burning flames and brimstone of the second death, wishing they never existed … forever! And for good measure, they will keep company with anyone not found written in the Book of Life (Revelation 20:15), Satan (Revelation 20:10), the beast and false prophet (Revelation 19:20), and Death and Hades (Revelation 20:14).

"*Then I saw another sign in heaven, great and marvelous: seven angels having the seven last plagues, for in them the wrath of God is complete*"

(Revelation 15:1). Just when you think the earth is hot enough as described above, God turns up the heat even more with the final bowl judgments. *"Then the fourth angel poured out his bowl on the sun, and power was given to him to scorch men with fire"* (Revelation 16:8). Ouch! The wrath on the unrighteous, prophesied by our Creator in His Word, will be complete. The second resurrection at the end of the millennial reign of Christ awaits, with their future eternal destiny being the lake of fire.

"For a fire is kindled in My anger, and shall burn to the lowest hell; it shall consume the earth with her increase, and set on fire the foundations of the mountains" (Deuteronomy 32:22). Climate change is coming! Global warming is imminent! It will be God-made and remake the heavens and earth. Get ready now and ask Jesus to be your Savior or repent and get back into a right relationship with Him.

Chapter Six
CO_2

At the time of this writing, the following statement was posted on the website for the United States Environmental Protection Agency (EPA): "It is not too late to have a significant impact on future climate change and its effects on us. With appropriate actions by governments, communities, individuals, and businesses, we can reduce the amount of greenhouse gas pollution we release and lower the risk of much greater warming and severe consequences. Many of the actions that we can take to address climate change will have other benefits, such as cleaner, healthier air. In addition, communities can take action to prepare for the changes we know are coming." A quick rebuff to this statement is "*I have seen all the works that are done under the sun; and indeed, all is vanity and grasping for the wind*" (Ecclesiastes 1:14). The EPA's premise is that man can control what God created. There is nothing man can create, repurpose or invent without using God's resources. In other words, it is not possible to create your own dirt! *"There is nothing new under the sun"* (Ecclesiastes 1:9). It is simply not possible for man to create something out of nothing. So it all comes back to this one important question, "Would a sovereign Creator create humanity to inhabit His creation knowing that humans have the power to destroy it?" No! So what is this really about?

We already discussed idolatry being the root cause, which is worshipping creation instead of the Creator. But this chapter digs deeper. The "climate change" movement has become a religion based on emotion, ignorance, propaganda and monetary agendas. *"No one can serve two masters; for either he will hate the one and love the other, or else he will be loyal to the one and despise the other. You cannot serve God and mammon"* (Matthew 6:24). Mammon is translated as avarice (extreme greed for wealth or material gain). There will come a day when you will be taxed on the air you breathe or if you have farm animals, taxed on the air they breathe! Why? Because you will be convinced that you are causing "climate change" and polluting the earth, so to help offset the effects, you need to pay your fair share. Sound crazy? I assure you it is not far-fetched. Jesus concluded His "parable of the unrighteous steward" by stating in Matthew 6:34, *"Therefore do not worry about tomorrow, for tomorrow will worry about its own things."* Worry is a sin. God is in control and always will be. We have enough things that garner our attention and what God created and controls should not be one of them, let alone being taxed on it.

With that said, proponents will show you propaganda pictures of polar bears floating on ice, melting glaciers, damage and/or loss of life from storms, earthquakes and volcanoes. This is done to invoke the impulse emotion of fear so you will do something to help stop "climate change." *"For God has not given us a spirit of fear, but of power and of love and of a sound mind"* (2 Timothy 1:7). It is one thing to have compassion on others and meet their needs when something tragic happens. It is another thing to think you can prevent what God controls. Use your sound mind and judgment when it comes to such matters. American theologian Reinhold Niebuhr said it best: "God, grant me the serenity to accept the things I cannot change, courage to change the things I can, and wisdom to know the difference."

After reading this chapter, ignorance will no longer be an excuse either.

Carbon dioxide (CO_2) is a colorless and odorless gas vital to life on earth. It is vital because God created it for plant life and all living things that breathe. "*Thus says God the LORD, Who created the heavens and stretched them out, Who spread forth the earth and that which comes from it, Who gives breath to the people on it, and spirit to those who walk on it*" (Isaiah 42:5). We need God to breathe, for He is the source of it! He does not need us, or the EPA's help to reverse or stop something He controls. "*Nor is He worshiped with men's hands, as though He needed anything, since He gives to all life, breath, and all things*" (Acts 17:25). Natural sources for carbon dioxide (CO_2) include volcanoes, hot springs and geysers and it is freed from carbonate rocks by dissolution in water and acids. Since CO_2 is soluble in water, it occurs naturally in groundwater, rivers and lakes, in ice caps and glaciers and in seawater. It is present in deposits of petroleum and natural gas. God made all of it!

As part of the carbon cycle, plants, algae, and certain bacteria use light energy to photosynthesize carbohydrates from carbon dioxide and water, with oxygen produced as a waste product. Conversely, CO_2 is a product of respiration. It is returned to water via the gills of fish and to the air via the lungs of air-breathing land animals, including humans. Only a creative genius could have created such a cycle, one that includes the sun, earth, water, plants, trees, fish, animals and humans. That would be God, our Creator. Carbon dioxide is produced during the processes of decay of organic materials and the fermentation of sugars in bread, beer and winemaking. *"Our fathers ate the manna in the desert; as it is written, 'He gave them bread from heaven to eat'"* (John 6:31). God sustained the children of Israel with manna for forty years (Exodus 16:35). Should we have taxed God for this process? Jesus is the bread of life (John 6:33, 35, 48, 51) and one day we will eat manna in heaven with Him at His table: *"To him who overcomes I will give some of the hidden manna to eat"* (Revelation 2:17). Yes, we still eat food in our resurrected bodies. Should we also tax Jesus for turning water into wine (John 2:1-10), since it too must have produced CO_2?

Carbon dioxide is produced by combustion of wood, carbohydrates and fossil fuels such as coal, peat, petroleum and natural gas. *"Then, as soon as they had come to land, they saw a fire of coals there, and fish laid on it, and bread"* (John 21:9). Jesus appeared to the disciples after His resurrection a third time on the shore of the Tiberias Sea. He had started a fire of coals to prepare breakfast for Himself and His disciples. Oh, the inhumanity of it all! CO_2 comes from the production of bread and from the burning of coals. Keep in mind that Jesus is the reason why all things exists – visible and invisible (Colossians 1:16). Carbon dioxide is used for welding, fire extinguishers, air guns, oil recovery, chemical feedstock, food additive (a candy called "Pop Rocks" is pressurized with carbon dioxide gas), and to decaffeinate coffee. It is added to drinking water and carbonated beverages, including beer, champagne and soda. Look out soda makers, you will be taxed one day for CO_2. The frozen solid form of CO_2 (known as "dry ice") is used as a refrigerant and as an abrasive in dry-ice blasting. We are surrounded by CO_2 from all angles and we are to believe man is causing "global warming" and/or "climate change" because of something God created for our survival and use? "*You take away their breath, they die and return to their dust*" (Psalm 104:29). God controls His creation.

Organic oils are produced by plants, animals, and other organisms through natural metabolic processes. "*And you shall command the children of Israel that they bring you pure oil of pressed olives for the light, to cause the lamp to burn continually*" (Exodus 27:20). Lipid is the scientific term for the fatty acids, steroids and similar chemicals often found in the oils produced by living things, while oil refers to an overall mixture of chemicals. Lipids have a high carbon and hydrogen content. Crude oil, or petroleum, and its refined components are crucial resources in the modern economy. Crude oil originates from ancient fossilized organic materials. The name "mineral oil" is a misnomer, in that minerals are not the source of the oil—ancient plants and animals are. Therefore, mineral oil (coming from unknown source in rocks) is also organic. "*He made him draw honey from the rock, and oil from the flinty rock*" (Deuteronomy 32:13). There is nothing under the sun that is new! God created everything and thus controls everything. Man can only repurpose what God created.

"*I will show wonders in heaven above and signs in the earth beneath: blood and fire and vapor of smoke*" (Acts 2:19). As the previous chapter can attest to, God-made global warming is coming. All the fire rained down on earth will cause an exorbitant amount of carbon dioxide to be released into the air. "*And he opened the bottomless pit, and smoke arose out of the pit like the smoke of a great furnace. So the sun and the air were darkened because of the smoke of the pit*" (Revelation 9:2). The smoke will be so thick that it will be difficult to breathe outside, if you are not killed by the fire itself. "*Smoke went up from His nostrils, and devouring fire from His mouth; coals were kindled by it*" (Psalm 18:8). But even with all that said, the current earth will remain (having been cleansed) and produce a millennial atmosphere of peace where Christ and His bride rule and reign with humanity with a rod of iron (Revelation 2:26-27). The EPA can do nothing to stop or prevent what God has ordained for His Son, Jesus Christ. The EPA can propagate a false narrative, with the help of the United States Department of Education, to indoctrinate our children into thinking humans are causing "climate change." Both agencies need to be done away with … today!

"*For the life of the flesh is in the blood, and I have given it to you upon the altar to make atonement for your souls; for it is the blood that makes atonement for the soul*" (Leviticus 17:11). The ultimate atonement was made by Jesus. "*Not with the blood of goats and calves, but with His own blood He entered the Most Holy Place once for all, having obtained eternal redemption*" (Hebrews 9:12). So not only is life in the blood (that means a baby in the womb is life), but eternal life is in the blood of Jesus. Guess what else is in the blood? Carbon dioxide! CO_2 is carried in blood in three different ways. Hemoglobin, the main oxygen-carrying molecule in red blood cells, carries both oxygen and carbon dioxide. A person's breathing rate influences the level of CO_2 in their blood. Although the body requires oxygen for metabolism, low oxygen levels normally do not stimulate breathing. Rather, breathing is stimulated by higher carbon dioxide levels. The body produces approximately 2.3 pounds of carbon dioxide per day per person. This carbon dioxide is carried through the venous system and is breathed out through the lungs. God, our Creator, created our intricate bodies to function perfectly. Of course sin in the world put a temporary damper on things causing each one of us to die physically.

Do you want to be directly taxed on the air you breathe? Indirectly, we are taxed today through a "carbon tax" on the things we consume and products we buy. Companies have to pass that cost to the consumer or they would go out of business, which is sometimes the goal of the proponents of climate change (those who worship creation over the Creator). As of this writing, the following is taken from the Center for Climate and Energy Solutions: "A carbon tax uses the power of market price signals to encourage greenhouse gas emission reductions from a variety of sources. The predominant greenhouse gas produced by humans is carbon dioxide (CO_2), which results largely from burning fossil fuels. An upstream carbon tax, for example, would impose a charge on coal, oil, and natural gas in proportion to the amount of carbon they contain. This tax would be passed forward into the price of electricity, petroleum products, and energy-intensive goods. A more broad-based carbon tax could also be designed to apply to non-energy sources of CO_2 emissions and on other greenhouse gases based on their global warming potential relative to CO_2. The burning of fossil fuels and other activities that release greenhouse gases are associated with warming global temperatures and adverse climate impacts. The costs of these impacts, including an increase in extreme and damaging weather events, rising sea levels, loss of biodiversity and other effects, will be borne by society as a whole, including future generations."

One word comes to mind – indoctrination. And you wonder why your electric bill and car payments are so high. The only way this madness stops is to educate others that God created this earth for our use. We are to be good stewards and take care of it. But once we cross the line of putting creation before the Creator, and then profit from it, you have created a false idolatrous religion. *"For they bind heavy burdens, hard to bear, and lay them on men's shoulders; but they themselves will not move them with one of their fingers. But all their works they do to be seen by men"* (Matthew 23:4-5). Jesus was talking about the Scribes and Pharisees and how they created hundreds of additional laws (beyond what God said to Moses) for the Jewish people that, they themselves, never kept nor intended to keep. He called them hypocrites (Matthew 23:13). Today, while we are being told to ride bikes and carpool to cut down on our carbon footprint, government officials fly across the world burning more fuel and money on one trip than most of us would ever do in a lifetime. Who's fooling who here? *"I do not set aside the grace of God; for if righteousness comes through the law, then Christ died in vain"* (Galatians 2:21). If you want to be saved, it is Jesus plus nothing! Once you are His, your desire with the help of the Holy Spirit will be to obey His commandments. But the laws of man will not make you righteous. Paying a carbon tax will not make you righteous, nor will it prevent "climate change" or "global warming." God the Father controls everything for the sole purpose of glorifying His Son. Now let's explore the last chapter to find out why.

Chapter Seven
Culmination

As stated previously, all of creation was created through, for and by Jesus Christ (Colossians 1:16), and served as a backdrop for a bigger purpose – good versus evil. "*To everything there is a season, a time for every purpose under heaven*" (Ecclesiastes 3:1). It is by God's will that creation exists. "*You are worthy, O Lord, to receive glory and honor and power; for You created all things, and by Your will they exist and were created*" (Revelation 4:11). Jesus said in Matthew 28:18, "*All authority has been given to Me in heaven and on earth.*" The earth will one day be inherited by King Jesus and His saints, those who believed in His name as their Savior (1 Thessalonians 3:13). "*Behold, the Lord comes with ten thousands of His saints*" (Jude 14). That is not possible if humanity, part of creation, has the power to completely destroy the earth before the day of the Lord.

"*That at the name of Jesus every knee should bow, of those in heaven, and of those on earth, and of those under the earth*" (Philippians 2:10). The reason why creation exists is for Jesus. Every single person will one day bow down to THE KING OF KINGS, AND LORD OF LORDS. The question is will you do it now or be forced to do it? "Now" leads to eternal life in heaven, the latter punches your ticket to the lake of fire. "*And many of those who sleep in the dust of the earth shall awake, some to everlasting life, some to shame and everlasting contempt*" (Daniel 12:2). But make no mistake, everyone will bow to the Creator. The spiritual battle between good and evil comes to a conclusion and the earth as we know it changes dramatically via fire a.k.a. God-made global warning. Then after the millennial reign of Christ, the current earth will pass away in favor of a new earth! "*For behold, I create new heavens and a new earth; and the former shall not be remembered or come to mind*" (Isaiah 65:17).

Let's discuss "evil" and how it came to be on this earth, for it is the main reason why the climate is cursed and changes constantly. Not only does our Creator control the natural physical world, He also maintains complete control of the spiritual realm. "*Put on the whole armor of God, that you may be able to stand against the wiles of the devil. For we do not wrestle against flesh and blood, but against principalities, against powers, against the rulers of the darkness of this age, against spiritual hosts of wickedness in the heavenly places"* (Ephesians 6:11-12). Eternal life aside, asking Jesus to be your Savior also bestows upon you His power via the Holy Spirit. *"Now hope does not disappoint, because the love of God has been poured out in our hearts by the Holy Spirit who was given to us"* (Romans 5:5). Without the armor of the Holy Spirit, you are simply vulnerable to the wiles (cunning arts, deceit, craft and trickery) of the devil. *"For Satan himself transforms himself into an angel of light"* (2 Corinthians 11:14).

Taken from Ezekiel 28:12-19, Lucifer was an anointed cherub (an angelic being) created for the purpose of serving God on His holy mountain, walking back and forth in the midst of fiery stones. Lucifer was the seal of perfection, full of wisdom, and perfect in beauty and in his ways from the day he was created. His physical covering included sardius, topaz, diamond, beryl, onyx, jasper, sapphire, turquoise, emerald, and gold. Lucifer became filled with violence, his heart filled with pride and his wisdom corrupted for the sake of his beauty and splendor. In other words Lucifer wanted God's glory. *"Pride goes before destruction, and a haughty spirit before a fall"* (Proverbs 16:18).

"So the great dragon was cast out, that serpent of old, called the Devil and Satan, who deceives the

whole world; he was cast to the earth, and his angels were cast out with him" (Revelation 12:9). Satan was cast out of where? The prophet Isaiah (14:12) emphatically tells us that Lucifer (translated as light-bearer, shining one or morning star) fell from heaven, where God's throne resides (2 Corinthians 12:2), to the earth: "*How you are fallen from heaven, O Lucifer, son of the morning!*" Jesus, the only begotten Son of God (John 3:16), witnessed the expulsion, confirming He existed from the beginning of time, being the Alpha and the Omega (Revelation 1:8). "*And He said to them, 'I saw Satan fall like lightning from heaven'*" (Luke 10:18). Now you know why the serpent was on earth to tempt Eve. "*You were in Eden, the garden of God*" (Ezekiel 28:13). The Book of Job (1:7; 2:2) confirms Satan today walks to and fro on the earth, seeking whom he may devour on this cursed earth (1 Peter 5:8).

Now let's discuss "good" and how it will make all things new again, the ultimate climate change. Unlike Adam, who was created as an adult from dust, Jesus came to earth as a baby, born via the Holy Spirit within the virgin womb of a Jewish mother named Mary (Matthew 1:18). After eight days from birth, Jesus was circumcised according to the Torah (Leviticus 12:3; Luke 2:21). His parents went to Jerusalem every year at the Feast of the Passover and took him along until He came of age (Luke 2:41). Jesus ultimately became the Passover Lamb of God on the cross. At the age of twelve, He was teaching among teachers in the Jewish temple (Luke 2:42-50). When Jesus started His ministry, one of His recruited disciples called Him Rabbi, Son of God and King of Israel (John 1:49). Jesus never rebuked him. *"Concerning His Son Jesus Christ our Lord, who was born of the seed of David according to the flesh"* (Romans 1:3).

Israel is God's firstborn son of inheritance among nations (Exodus 4:22). Do not confuse this with Jesus being the only begotten Son of God. Christians are also called sons and daughters. *"I will be a Father to you, and you shall be My sons and daughters, says the Lord Almighty"* (2 Corinthians 6:18). But Israel has firstborn rights, in this case inheritance to land with the earthly temple of God being in Jerusalem, God's chosen city (Matthew 5:35). Since God is the Creator of the earth, He can give land to whomever He wants. *"On the same day the Lord made a covenant with Abram, saying: 'To your descendants I have given this land, from the river of Egypt to the great river, the River Euphrates'"* (Genesis 15:18). God has given landmarks and a deeded title for the land to Abraham's descendants forever. God would never forsake His children.

A believer's works is judged by fire (1 Corinthians 3:12-15). "*For we must all appear before the judgment seat of Christ, that each one may receive the things done in the body, according to what he has done, whether good or bad*" (2 Corinthians 5:10). All sinners saved by grace appear in heaven at the judgement seat of Christ. "*For by grace you have been saved through faith, and that not of yourselves; it is the gift of God*" (Ephesians 2:8). The judgment seat is for all who experience the first resurrection, as discussed in previous chapters. Our sins are judged at the cross, but our works are judged in heaven before King Jesus. Each one will receive the things done in the body after being saved by the blood of Jesus. "*If anyone's work which he has built on it endures, he will receive a reward*" (1 Corinthians 3:14). The fire will reveal who receives rewards and who doesn't. This works judgment precedes the millennial earthly reign of Christ and His Saints. Note that Jesus does not redistribute the rewards among His Saints so all have the same amount. Would it be fair that someone who has given their life to the Lord since their teenage years receive the same rewards as someone who accepts Jesus on their death bed? Of course not! "*And behold, I am coming quickly, and My reward is with Me, to give to every one according to his work*" (Revelation 22:12). Heaven is the ultimate reward for all believers, but God still has a hierarchy of responsibility during His earthly reign. "*And I saw thrones, and they sat on them, and judgment was committed to them*" (Revelation 20:4). Who does what and where is His to be determined. "*And have made us kings and priests to our God; and we shall reign on the earth*" (Revelation 5:10).

As chapter five explains, the cursed earth is reserved for fire (2 Peter 3:5-7). As the Book of Revelation reveals, the twenty-one plagues dished out on His creation kills one-third of the population and remakes the overall landscape of the earth so new growth can begin. The events that reshape the earth are completely controlled by our Creator. Nothing man does will prevent or reverse climate change or stop the spiritual battle between good and evil. "*Now I saw heaven opened, and behold, a white horse. And He who sat on him was called Faithful and True, and in righteousness He judges and makes war*" (Revelation 19:11). That would be King Jesus – the reason why all creation exists! The war will be against the antichrist (the beast), the kings of the earth, and their armies (Revelation 19:19). They have come to attack the nation of Israel and in effect make war against Him who sat on the horse and against His army. *"He was clothed with a robe dipped in blood, and His name is called The Word of God. And the armies in heaven, clothed in fine linen, white and clean, followed Him on white horses"* (Revelation 19:13-14). His army is the church, all which believed in the name of Jesus Christ for their salvation. Every single one of them are now in their resurrected bodies, in the likeness of their Savior.

"Now out of His mouth goes a sharp sword, that with it He should strike the nations. And He Himself will rule them with a rod of iron. He Himself treads the winepress of the fierceness and wrath of Almighty God" (Revelation 19:15). Pardon the expression, but Satan and his followers don't have a prayer to win this war. *"For behold, the Lord is coming out of His place; He will come down and tread on the high places of the earth"* (Micah 1:3). The fiery strike from the Lord will be so quick and intense, the prophet Zechariah described it this way: *"And this shall be the plague with which the Lord will strike all the people who fought against Jerusalem: Their flesh shall dissolve while they stand on their feet, their eyes shall dissolve in their sockets, and their tongues shall dissolve in their mouths"* (Zechariah 14:12). That same supernatural fire will not harm the people of Israel (Isaiah 43:2).

"*Then the beast was captured, and with him the false prophet who worked signs in his presence, by which he deceived those who received the mark of the beast and those who worshiped his image. These two were cast alive into the lake of fire burning with brimstone. And the rest were killed with the sword which proceeded from the mouth of Him who sat on the horse*" (Revelation 19:20-21). The antichrist and false prophet were cast alive into the lake of fire, not to be confused with Hades beneath the earth.

"*Then I saw an angel coming down from heaven, having the key to the bottomless pit and a great chain in his hand. He laid hold of the dragon, that serpent of old, who is the Devil and Satan, and bound him for a thousand years; and he cast him into the bottomless pit, and shut him up, and set a seal on him, so that he should deceive the nations no more till the thousand years were finished. But after these things he must be released for a little while*" (Revelation 20:1-3). It has to irritate Satan, a past anointed cherub, tremendously that God uses another angel to lay hold of him and bound him for a thousand years. Both Satan and the fallen angels are reserved for judgment. "*And the angels who did not keep their proper domain, but left their own abode, He has reserved in everlasting chains under darkness for the judgment of the great day*" (Jude 6).

It is interesting that God chose to bind Satan in the earth instead of casting him into the lake of fire with his evil agents, the antichrist and false prophet. That is because sin still exists and humans still die during the millennial reign of Christ. People will still have "free will" to choose or reject Jesus, whom they will be able to see with their own eyes! The only difference is they don't have a pest to tempt them during the millennial reign. Adam and Eve (the only ones made in the image of God) never had that privilege. There will be no serpent to come along and tempt them to eat some forbidden fruit. Yet sadly, some humans will reject Jesus just as Lucifer and the angels that followed him did. As you can see, created angels also have "free will" to worship and serve their Creator, God the Father. The big difference between them and humans is that fallen angels have no path of redemption. That privilege is only for humans through the blood of Jesus. Angels already knew who Jesus was from the beginning and they still chose to reject Him. Pride will do that to you.

"Heaven is My throne, and earth is My footstool" (Isaiah 66:1; Acts 7:49). *"And the Lord shall be King over all the earth"* (Zechariah 14:9). *"Your kingdom come. Your will be done on earth as it is in heaven"* (Matthew 6:10). So what is creation like during

the millennial reign? One thing is for sure, the climate and the earth will have dramatically changed by the hand of God. *"And in that day His feet will stand on the Mount of Olives, which faces Jerusalem on the east. And the Mount of Olives shall be split in two, from east to west, making a very large valley; half of the mountain shall move toward the north and half of it toward the south"* (Zechariah 14:4). Jesus will come back to Jerusalem to rule on the throne of King David, for He is the Lion of the tribe of Judah (Revelation 5:5). *"Has in these last days spoken to us by His Son, whom He has appointed heir of all things, through whom also He made the worlds"* (Hebrews 1:2). Through marriage (Revelation 19:7), Jesus and His bride are joint heirs to all things. *"The Spirit Himself bears witness with our spirit that we are children of God, and if children, then heirs—heirs of God and joint heirs with Christ, if indeed we suffer with Him, that we may also be glorified together"* (Romans 8:16-17). We brought our filthy rags (Isaiah 64:6) and laid it at His feet and in return He forgave us, cleansed us and bestowed upon us all that He owns. What a bargain!

"The wolf also shall dwell with the lamb, and the leopard shall lie down with the kid; and the calf and the young lion and the fatling together; and a little child shall lead them" (Isaiah 11:6). Can you

102

picture the little child walking his or her lion and taking a nap on the belly of a leopard? That will happen during the millennial reign as animals no longer fear humans and diets revert back to fruits and vegetation. "*The cow and the bear shall graze; their young ones shall lie down together; and the lion shall eat straw like the ox. The nursing child shall play by the cobra's hole, and the weaned child shall put his hand in the viper's den. They shall not hurt nor destroy in all My holy mountain, for the earth shall be full of the knowledge of the LORD as the waters cover the sea*" (Isaiah 11:7-9). God gives us a glimpse of what He intended for creation in the garden of Eden. "*And in that day it shall be that living waters shall flow from Jerusalem*" (Zechariah 14:8). No one will ever thirst again.

As for the nations which came against Jerusalem in war, everyone left must go to Jerusalem from year to year to worship the King, the Lord of hosts, and to keep the Feast of Tabernacles. And if they do not, on them there will be no rain for that year (Zechariah 14:16-17). God maintains complete control of His creation and rules the earth, along with His bride, with a rod of iron. "*Unto us a Son is given; and the government will be upon His shoulder*" (Isaiah 9:6). No more will there be ungodly laws for a thousand years that are contrary to the Word of

God. Since rain still exists, so does seedtime and harvest (Genesis 8:22). "*They shall build houses and inhabit them; they shall plant vineyards and eat their fruit. They shall not build and another inhabit; they shall not plant and another eat ... and My elect shall long enjoy the work of their hands*" (Isaiah 65:21-22). There will be no war or disputes over land during this period, wherein someone else takes property by force. There will be no taxes on labor or property! "*They shall not labor in vain, nor bring forth children for trouble*" (Isaiah 65:23). Many children will be born during this time of peace. For as the days of a tree, so shall be the days of His people be (Isaiah 65:22). "*No more shall an infant from there live but a few days, nor an old man who has not fulfilled his days; for the child shall die one hundred years old, but the sinner being one hundred years old shall be accursed*" (Isaiah 65:20). The lifespan for those who choose Jesus as Savior during this period could last as the days of a tree, well past one hundred years. By comparison, Methuselah lived to be 969 (Genesis 5:27). It is conceivable that some humans will live to the very end of the millennial reign. For those who reject Jesus, they will be accursed (the curse of death) and escorted to Hades.

Speaking of Hades, let's explore the different terms used in the Bible that describes the underworld. The word "hell" encompasses many terms found in scripture. In the Old Testament the words "grave," "hell" and "pit" occur sixty-five times in conjunction with the Hebrew root word "Sheol." The terms "grave" and "hell" can also be found in the New Testament. That is because the curse of a physical death still exists for all. Sheol is never used in the New Testament because it is now empty. What caused the changed? The death, resurrection and ascension of Jesus Christ.

The current earth today is an incubator for Hades. However, prior to the miracle of the cross, Sheol was a temporary holding place for the righteous dead (the place of departed souls/spirits). In 1 Samuel 28, Saul (Israel's first King) asked a woman medium to conduct a séance so that he could talk with Samuel (Israel's last Judge), who had recently died. "*And the woman said to Saul, 'I saw a spirit ascending out of the earth'*" (1 Samuel 28:13). Samuel even confirmed that he was brought up from the earth: "*Now Samuel said to Saul, 'Why have you disturbed me by bringing me up?'*" (1 Samuel 28:15). So where was Samuel? He was in Sheol. King David prophesied that his soul, nor the Messiah's soul would be left in Sheol: "*For You will not leave my soul in Sheol, nor will You allow*

Your Holy One to see corruption" (Psalm 16:10).

The New Testament uses the term "Hades" when referring to the realm of the dead, grave or hell. In scripture, the term "hell" is used to describe both Sheol and Hades. Both Sheol (Job 17:16; Isaiah 38:10) and Hades have gates (Matthew 16:18). Jesus is the only one who has the keys to the gates of Hades: "*And I have the keys of Hades and of Death*" (Revelation 1:18). Since Sheol is now empty, the keys for its gates have already been used. "*When He ascended on high, He led captivity captive — what does it mean but that He also first descended into the lower parts of the earth? He who descended is also the One who ascended far above all the heavens, that He might fill all things*" (Ephesians 4:8-10). When Jesus died, He descended into the lower parts of the earth and preached to the spirits in prison (1 Peter 3:19). That prison was Sheol, the temporary holding place for the righteous dead. The message preached from Jesus was to proclaim that death, hell and the grave have been defeated. If you recall, the first wave of the first resurrection happened in the streets of Jerusalem after His resurrection (Matthew 27:51-53). Many were astonished at the dead now walking around alive in their new bodies.

Also within the earth is a bottomless pit with

one key. "*And I saw a star fallen from heaven to the earth. To him was given the key to the bottomless pit*" (Revelation 9:1). The angel of the bottomless pit has a name, Apollyon, otherwise known as the Destroyer (Revelation 9:11). In Revelation 20:1, that angel throws Satan into the bottomless pit, bound for one thousand years. Some people also think that the angels who followed Lucifer and left their proper domain are also bound with everlasting chains in the bottomless pit (Jude 6). But where is the bottomless pit in conjunction with Hades?

Jesus Christ fills in some of the mystery through "The Rich Man and Lazarus" parable in Luke 16:19-31. In your mind draw a big circle representing hell. Now draw two lines parallel to each other in the middle of the circle representing the gulf, or a gaping opening. "*And besides all this, between us and you there is a great gulf fixed, so that those who want to pass from here to you cannot, nor can those from there pass to us*" (Luke 16:26). It is my opinion that this gulf or chasm with one key is the bottomless pit. Now you have two additional sections within the circle. "*So it was that the beggar died, and was carried by the angels to Abraham's bosom. The rich man also died and was buried*" (Luke 16:22). Abraham is the father of all who believe

(Romans 4:16), thus Abraham's bosom is the section called "Sheol" in the Old Testament. The rich man was just buried and angels carried him to the opposite section of hell. "*And being in torments in Hades, he lifted up his eyes and saw Abraham afar off, and Lazarus in his bosom*" (Luke 16:23). Note again that the presence of God is everywhere. "*If I ascend into heaven, You are there; If I make my bed in hell, behold, You are there*" (Psalm 139:8). Part of being tormented is being able to see what could have been and never attaining it. Abraham and Lazarus were in Sheol, on the other side of the gulf, being comforted. Today Sheol is empty and all that is left is the bottomless pit and Hades for the unrighteous dead.

Today, giving your life to Jesus assures that your soul makes a beeline to heaven awaiting the resurrection of your new body. "*We are confident, yes, well pleased rather to be absent from the body and to be present with the Lord*" (2 Corinthians 5:8). In Revelation 6:9-11, God gives us a glimpse of what happens to the souls of the righteous upon death. The Fifth Seal tells us that souls are preserved under the altar of God, given white robes and in a state of rest awaiting the resurrection. For believers, death no longer has a sting to it (1 Corinthians 15:55). "*O Death, where is* your sting? O Hades, where is your victory?" King David said it best: "*Yea, though I walk through the valley of the shadow of death, I will fear no evil; for You are with me; Your rod and Your staff, they comfort me*" (Psalm 23:4). A shadow never hurt anyone.

On the opposite end of the spectrum, Jesus continues the story of the rich man. An unbeliever's soul at death goes to Hades in a tormented flame (Luke 16:24). "*If your hand causes you to sin, cut it off. It is better for you to enter into life maimed, rather than having two hands, to go to hell, into the fire that shall never be quenched—where 'Their worm does not die and the fire is not quenched'*" (Mark 9:43-44). Ouch! "*And he cried and said, Father Abraham, have mercy on me, and send Lazarus, that he may dip the tip of his finger in water, and cool my tongue; for I am tormented in this flame*" (Luke 16:24). If only he could taste the coolness of living water again. Those in Hades are also aware of their surroundings, with their thoughts tormented by family members still living who may not be saved. "*Then he said, 'I beg you therefore, father, that you would send him to my father's house, for I have five brothers, that he may testify to them, lest they also come to this place of torment'*" (Luke 16:27-28). What the rich man found out upon death is that

Hades is a real place, whether he believed it or not.

"Now when the thousand years have expired, Satan will be released from his prison and will go out to deceive the nations which are in the four corners of the earth ... to gather them together to battle, whose number is as the sand of the sea" (Revelation 20:7-8). Those who refused to worship Jesus toward the end of the millennial reign will easily follow Satan. If one could learn anything from Satan, it is persistence. You would think he learned his lesson from the battle won by King Jesus before the reign, but no. So God teaches him one final lesson. *"They went up on the breadth of the earth and surrounded the camp of the saints and the beloved city. And fire came down from God out of heaven and devoured them"* (Revelation 20:9). The angels of God then take care of Satan for good. *"The devil, who deceived them, was cast into the lake of fire and brimstone where the beast and the false prophet are. And they will be tormented day and night forever and ever"* (Revelation 20:10). Those who followed him died instantly on the spot and were escorted to Hades.

To all the environmentalists, manmade "global warming" and "climate change" proponents, and those who worship creation or "Mother Earth" – our Creator will create something new and do away with the old. "*Heaven and earth will pass away, but My words will by no means pass away*" (Matthew 24:35). The main purpose for creation is reaching its culmination. This earth and heaven will perish, being folded up like a cloak (Hebrews 1:10-12). All the mortal believers during the reign will be translated into their new bodies in the twinkling of an eye, just as their predecessors were (1 Thessalonians 4:17). "*For this corruptible must put on incorruption, and this mortal must put on immortality*" (1 Corinthians 15:53). The city of God will be replaced with many mansions, discussed more below. "*In My Father's house are many mansions; if it were not so, I would have told you*" (John 14:2).

For unbelievers in Hades, it just got worse! "*Then I saw a great white throne and Him who sat on it, from whose face the earth and the heaven fled away. And there was found no place for them*" (Revelation 20:11). Once the earth and heaven (the sky) are folded up, Hades is emptied. "*The sea gave up the dead who were in it, and Death and Hades delivered up the dead who were in them*" (Revelation 20:13). The second resurrection takes place for the unrighteous dead. Suspended somewhere between the highest heaven and what use to be earth is a great white throne with the KING OF KINGS, AND LORD OF LORDS sitting on it ready to judge! "*And I saw the dead, small and great, standing before God, and books were opened. And another book was opened, which is the Book of Life. And the dead were judged according to their works, by the things which were written in the books. And they were judged, each one according to his works*" (Revelation 20:12-13). The Book of Life is opened to simply show something is missing – their names. There is a pay day some day and this last day is it! The only way to guarantee your name in the Book of Life is to believe in Jesus as your Savior. In Hades it is too late and at this last judgment it is way too late! Just as all those who were saved appeared before Jesus in heaven (1 Corinthians 3:12-15) so that their works could be tried by fire (for the purpose of rewards), the same works judgment will happen to the unrighteous before being escorted to the lake of fire.

Jesus will open "books" and each one will give an account for his or her works. "*But the cowardly, unbelieving, abominable, murderers, sexually immoral, sorcerers, idolaters, and all liars shall have their part in the lake which burns with fire and brimstone, which is the second death*" (Revelation 21:8). The key word above is "unbelieving!" Because of unbelief in Jesus, you will pay the penalty for sin ... again. "*For the* wages of sin is death, but the gift of God is eternal life in Christ Jesus our Lord" (Romans 6:23). By not accepting Jesus' substitutionary death on your behalf for your sins, now your newly resurrected body will experience a second death and pay the debt owed. "*Then Death and Hades were cast into the lake of fire. This is the second death. And anyone not found written in the Book of Life was cast into the lake of fire*" (Revelation 20:14-15).

"*Now I saw a new heaven and a new earth, for the first heaven and the first earth had passed away. Also there was no more sea. Then I, John, saw the holy city, New Jerusalem, coming down out of heaven from God, prepared as a bride adorned for her husband.*" (Revelation 21:1-2). Hallelujah, the mansions have arrived! God is making His creation all new without sin in the world. "*And God will wipe away every tear from their eyes; there shall be no more death, nor sorrow, nor crying. There shall be no more pain, for the former things have passed away. Then He who sat on the throne said, 'Behold, I make all things new'*" (Revelation 21:4-5). The Lord God Almighty (the Father) and the Lamb (Jesus) are its temple. "*The city had no need of the sun or of the moon to shine in it, for the glory of God illuminated it. The Lamb is its light*" (Revelation 21:23). How's that for climate change?!

The light shining through the city was like a jasper stone, clear as crystal. The city had great and high walls with twelve gates, and twelve angels at the gates, and names written on them, which are the names of the twelve tribes of the children of Israel (representing the Old Testament). *"The twelve gates were twelve pearls: each individual gate was of one pearl. And the street of the city was pure gold, like transparent glass"* (Revelation 21:23). The construction of its wall was of jasper; and the city was pure gold, like clear glass. The foundations of the wall were adorned with twelve precious stones, having on them the names of the twelve apostles of the Lamb (representing the New Testament). It is amazing that Jesus, a carpenter by trade on earth, would continue His carpentry work in heaven creating this masterpiece for you and me!

"The city is laid out as a square; its length is as great as its breadth. And he measured the city with the reed: twelve thousand furlongs. Its length, breadth, and height are equal. Then he measured its wall: one hundred and forty-four cubits" (Revelation 21:16-17). First, the wall is seventy-two yards (144 cubits) thick. Twelve thousand furlongs is 1500 miles, which means the city is 1500 square miles in length, debt and height. The world's

tallest manmade structure is the 2,722-foot tall Burj Khalifa in Dubai, United Arab Emirates. That equates to a little more than half a mile high, which means you would have to stack on top of each other approximately 3000 of the tallest building in the world, the Burj Khalifa, to reach the height of the New Jerusalem. Then put side by side horizontally 3000 more of them to reach the length and yet another 3000 more to reach the depth. What is even more astounding is that space is only 62 miles from the earth's surface. You have to travel another 1438 more miles (equivalent to driving from Miami, Florida to Albany, New York) to see the top of the New Jerusalem. Many mansions on high indeed... wow!

Lastly, the tree of life from the beginning days of the garden of Eden makes a second debut. *"And he showed me a pure river of water of life, clear as crystal, proceeding from the throne of God and of the Lamb. In the middle of its street, and on either side of the river, was the tree of life, which bore twelve fruits, each tree yielding its fruit every month. The leaves of the tree were for the healing of the nations"* (Revelation 22:1-2). We will drink from the river of life and eat from the tree of life. There shall be no more curse and we shall reign forever and ever. Good wins over evil.

"Who has ascended into heaven, or descended? Who has gathered the wind in His fists? Who has bound the waters in a garment? Who has established all the ends of the earth? What is His name, and what is His Son's name, if you know?" (Proverbs 30:4). If you don't know the answer, re-read this book again. *"For God is the King of all the earth"* (Psalm 47:7).

Man-made "global warming" and "climate change" is simply a farce. It is time we heed what the word of God, the Bible, discloses about creation and the Creator. That is what this book tried to accomplish through prayer, guidance, research and study. It is the environmentalists who worship creation over the Creator. While we are to be good stewards of the earth, we lose sight that we are also His creation. Why would a Creator, God, create mankind to inhabit His creation knowing that man has the power to destroy His creation? He wouldn't and He didn't. The "climate change" movement is an idolatrous religion based on emotion, ignorance, propaganda and monetary agendas. I have done my best to set the record straight through the Word of God. I implore you, worship the Creator instead of His creation.

www.ingramcontent.com/pod-product-compliance
Lightning Source LLC
Chambersburg PA
CBHW031517040426
42445CB00009B/275